This is a book you can use now, five years from now, and for all of your life. It is relevant wherever you are in your growth and development, even when you need to stop, go back, redo, and recycle life lessons.

It doesn't matter what path you have chosen, what starting place you find yourself in. You may be Buddhist, Hindu, Jewish, or Christian. It is up to you how comfortable you are as a participant in those teachings. Each of them contains the universal truths, though said and practiced in different ways.

My religious background is Disciples of Christ and Unity. I learned in both of them that God is Principle, though spoken of in different ways. My pathway is that of the disciple of clarity (Christos) and Unity.

The Divine Design

The Divine Design

How To Spiritually Interpret Your Life

Carole M. Lunde

iUniverse, Inc.
New York Lincoln Shanghai

The Divine Design
How To Spiritually Interpret Your Life

Copyright © 2007 by Carole M. Lunde

All rights reserved. No part of this book may be used or reproduced by any means, graphic, electronic, or mechanical, including photocopying, recording, taping or by any information storage retrieval system without the written permission of the publisher except in the case of brief quotations embodied in critical articles and reviews.

iUniverse books may be ordered through booksellers or by contacting:

iUniverse
2021 Pine Lake Road, Suite 100
Lincoln, NE 68512
www.iuniverse.com
1-800-Authors (1-800-288-4677)

Because of the dynamic nature of the Internet, any Web addresses or links contained in this book may have changed since publication and may no longer be valid.

The views expressed in this work are solely those of the author and do not necessarily reflect the views of the publisher, and the publisher hereby disclaims any responsibility for them.

ISBN: 978-0-595-43974-4 (pbk)
ISBN: 978-0-595-88294-6 (ebk)

Printed in the United States of America

TABLE OF CONTENTS

Introduction .... **xxi**

   1. How The Book Was Inspired xxi
       a. *By a profound question that had not yet been addressed.*
       b. *By my discovery that many spiritual students and teachers do not yet teach the spiritual interpretation of an individual lifetime.*
   2. What I Believe xxii
       a. *A listing of my beliefs about humanity and spirituality, with short explanations.*

Chapter One: **What Is Spiritual Interpretation** **1**

   1. What Is This Book About 1
       a. *Not about the psychic, karmic, ghoulish or strange, but who, what and why we are at any given moment.*
       b. *Investigating principles and ultimate reality. The study of Being.*
   2. What Is Real And What Isn't 2
       a. *Nature of the three-dimensional perspective*
       b. *Other dimensions of life, the "many mansions" mentioned by Jesus.*
       c. *Life more abundant through undiscovered potential.*
   3. Looking For The Spiritual Dimension 2
       a. *Pathways of light instead of dark psychic realms*
       b. *Being clear in our thinking through prayer*

4. What is Spiritual Interpretation? 3
   a. *Interpretation is a ladder of spiritual understanding that lifts us to a higher perception of our experience.*
   b. *2 Corinthians 5:16. "From now on we regard no one from a human point of view, but a divine one. Anyone in Christ is a new creation."*
5. Where Are We Going With This? 5
   a. *We are learning to be overcomers of our limited way of thinking.*
   b. *We are learning spiritual empowerment and godlikeness.*
   c. *The new dimension is soft and gentle, sweet and uplifting.*

Chapter Two: What Is In A Lifetime 7

1. Preparation for reading and working with the rest of the book. 7
   a. *Sketching out your life story*
   b. *Suggestions on how to do that*
   c. *Verbatim experiences from previous students*

Chapter Three: Getting to the Blessing 13

1. Why And How To Spiritually Interpret Your Life 13
   a. *We create a story from our own rationale of why things are the way they are, and how things work out for the best. It is a framework to make sense of our lives which honors the purpose of the intellect, and allows the intellect its rightful share in the process.*
   b. *We fill the intellectual framework with wisdom and learn to discern the difference.*
   c. *My rationale story is an example. How this helps us accomplish our mission on planet earth.*
   d. *Verbatim comments from students in class discussion.*

Chapter Four: Finding God's Threads, the Twelve Powers as listed by Charles Fillmore, Co-Founder of Unity, seen as threads

	we pull through our life experiences as we find them. 20
Chapter Five:	Faith—having faith that something good can and will happen. 23
Chapter Six :	Strength—becomes invincible through prayer. 25
Chapter Seven:	Wisdom—golden thread to lead to the heart of things 27
Chapter Eight:	Love—seems to dissolve in the face of materiality. 30
Chapter Nine:	Power—yank on or abuse this thread and it breaks some other threads. 32
Chapter Ten:	Imagination—colorful thread of creation 34
Chapter Eleven:	Understanding—brings compassion through the pattern 36
Chapter Twelve:	Will—from willful to willing 38
Chapter Thirteen:	Order—moving upon the unformed to bring the new order 40
Chapter Fourteen:	Zeal—fire to light up or to burn up your life 42
Chapter Fifteen:	Purification—discarding what is not Principle 44
Chapter Sixteen:	Life—eternal thread that never breaks 46

Chapter Seventeen: Creating Your Cosmic Story 48

1. There is more for us to experience than what we now know 48
   a. Why write your cosmic story
   b. Start preparing your place by writing a description of it.
   c. Self talk plays an important role

2. Some definitions 50
   a. A list of words that I use and what my definition for them is in this book.

   An invitation for the readers to create their own spiritual vocabulary that fits their personal needs.

   b. The importance of the new vocabulary in self-talk as we develop our new perspective.

Chapter Eighteen: Cosmic Stories By Former Students 53

1. Verbatim examples from students to help you get started 53
2. Beginning to write your own cosmic story. 56
   a. Step by step instructions

Chapter Nineteen: Getting Out Of The Swamp Of Confusion 59

1. Life experiences are confusing 59
   a. If we ruin the planet, where will we spend the money?
   b. Insanity of the ego created life experience as we know it.
   c. Trying to make sense of the ego created world can cause more insanity.

2. Helpful Clues 60
   a. Being in command of my behavior
   b. Who is right? Does right win? Right always wins at the spiritual level.

3. In Trying To Get Out, Or Out Trying to Get In? 61
   a. We are in it, but not of it.

4. Both Sides Now 62
   a. *The scope of our being includes physical and non-physical. Visible and invisible.*
   b. *We can understand at more than one level at a time.*

5. Power And Control 63
   a. *Physical level power and control are like riding a bronco. Sooner or later you will get thrown off.*
   b. *Spiritual words are empowerment and command. Empowerment of others and command of spiritual law practice.*

6. A Gift To Be Simple..63
   a. *Truth is simple. We create the confusion.*
   b. *Physical level of thinking causes confusion. Don't blame the level. Raise your thinking.*
   c. *Prayer returns us to simplicity and clarity. Psalms 26*

7. Application 65
   a. *Inventory of self-blame*
   b. *Suggestions for finding all the ways we blame ourselves.*
   c. *Use list to pray in the affirmative about each item.*

Chapter Twenty: God Bytes...67

1. Does God Really Talk To Me?..67
   a. *God gives us wisdom and information as we need it in ways we can understand.*
   b. *We learn to access what is already given.*

2. Flashes...67
   a. *A moment in consciousness when the door blows open.*

3. Hunches...68
   a. *Knowledge is always coming through at the level we are ready to receive. We just stumble into an open place from our foggy existence.*

4. Dreams 68
   a. Messages coming through the non-logical subconscious.
   b. Programming dreams by clearing the subconscious of negativity and causing it to run in a positive habit mode.

5. Guesses 70
   a. Building your confidence that you really do know!
   b. Exercising your innate wisdom.

6. The Open Channel 71
   a. We are naturally an open channel to God. Jesus was.
   b. Relying upon outer stuff causes us to close the channel and not trust it.
   c. Opening the channel we can receive megabytes and whole vistas of information.

7. Application 72
   a. Journal your God Bytes
   b. Suggestions for using this journal.

Chapter Twenty One: Making Sense Of Me..................74

1. Looking For God 74
   a. Trying to fill a void. I didn't know I was looking for God

2. Looking Out There 74
   a. Looking to romanticism, family, college majors.
   b. There were some clues.

3. Looking Inside 75
   a. Bingo! The light is within.
   b. Dig it out from the rubble of misunderstanding

4. "No" To Your Good 76
   a. What part of me says "no" to my good?
   b. What defeats all my good intentions?

5. Inside 77
   a. *The outside was a zigzag of events.*
   b. *The inside speaks.*
6. Saying "Yes" inside 78
   a. *Saying "yes" inside to our true nature*
   b. *Saying "yes" to living without old inner fears.*
   c. *Finding the tap root.*
   d. *Monster inside is a badly maligned angel.*
7. Inside Out 80
   a. *Bring the splendor from the inside to the outside.*
   b. *We can interface with God and bring it out.*
   c. *We can call it a miracle!*
8. Reaching In 81
   a. *Contemplation is reaching in.*
9. Application 82
   a. *Meditation*

Chapter Twenty Two: Finding Your Purpose 83

1. We Are Not Just Drifters In The Cosmos. 83
   a. *Your purpose came here with you*
   b. *You must access it by asking deep within.*
2. Use A Verb 84
   a. *Purpose has to do with serving the divine design in the arena of humanity.*
   b. *You are a qualified participant.*
3. We Are Here To Create 85
   a. *Wherever we are, we crate an energy pathway, and the material world mirrors for us what we cannot see.*
   b. *We can utilize all the pathways created so our energy can be focused upon our work. Jesus said, "I am the way ..."*

4. Your Message 86
   a. Levels of discovery of purpose in life experience.
   b. My sermon on the mount. Transformed are we ...
   c. Your sermon on the mount:

5. I Am My Quest 89
   a. Finding my purpose was my quest and expressing it through everything I do.
   b. Being on purpose is congruence, harmony and co-creation with God.

6. Activity 90
   a. Find a verb that describes your purpose.
   b. Beginning with that word, write your sermon on the mount.
   c. Suggestions on how to do this.

Chapter Twenty Three: Getting Into Heaven 92

1. Heaven Is Like 92
   a. References to Heaven in the Bible
   b. Heaven is a state of mind.
   c. Jesus' clues.

2. How Did We Get Out Of Heaven? 93
   a. We left our dimension as spiritual beings only to take on form.
   b. We got lost in appearances on the planet.
   c. Joy and happiness were considered frivolous

3. How Do We Stay Out? 94
   a. Our reality consists of whatever is appearing to us.
   b. We let the material world define us.

4. How Do We Get Back In? 94
   a. Happiness is a key. Not easy to find.
   b. We must learn to really see.

      c. The observer self.

      d. To the overcomers …

5. From Words To Silence 95

      a. Talking ourselves back into the silent place. Words drift away and we arrive on the threshold of the vast silent inner world.

6. Never Coming Back 96

      a. Life is progressive. We can't turn back in consciousness.

      b. Agony of leaving those who are unready, the ecstasy of knowing.

7. Heaven Is 96

      a. Heaven is knowing how to spiritually interpret your own life and experiences, finding the unlimited spiritual gift.

8. Adam and Eve 97

      a. Choosing co-creatorship with God.

      b. Learning to discern the invisible in the visible.

9. The Journey 97

      a. We chose to leave heaven to create heaven.

      b. We took a risk!

      c. Old Testament as the psychological development.

      d. New Testament as the spiritual development

10. Activity 99

Chapter Twenty Four: Asking For The Plan 100

1. Groping In The Dark For The Plan 100

      a. Everyone knows but me?

      b. The courage to ask.

2. Why Not Beg? 101

      a. Begging and beseeching are expressions of fear.

      b. The gift is already given.

3. Are We Arrogant? 101
   a. Arrogance is taking license in our fear-ridden ego state. Arrogance is meant to cover up fear.
4. How Should We Ask? 102
   a. Approach God in partnership and love.
5. Attitude is all 102
   a. Beliefs form attitudes
   b. Beliefs based upon spiritual truth form right attitudes.
6. Asking Is Claiming..103
   a. Asking God is equivalent to staking a claim for our good.
   b. Changing beliefs and attitudes takes time and work.
7. Activity 104
   a. Listing and sorting out attitudes and beliefs.

Chapter Twenty Five: What Is Your Part In The Greater Picture? 107

1. Fools Rush In..107
   a. Preparing for your part.
   b. Creating a divine space with guided meditation.
2. First, Stretching Exercises..108
   a. Mind-stretching ideas through study. The narrow single-channel mind is too limited.
3. Start By Stretching Self-Image...109
   a. Open up your wonderful fantasies about yourself.
   b. How to ask the question, "Who am I?"
   c. Spiritually, your greatest ideal is closest to the truth about you.
4. Who Is In Charge Of The Picture? 110
   a. Ultimately, you are the director, the producer, the script writer, the camera person.
   b. Great scenes come from great consciousness.

5. Think Big!...111
   a. A world of adventure.
   b. What it takes
6. What Is Your Theme?..113
   a. Finding the theme in your own heart.
   b. Looking at indicators.
   c. What are the stories I love and what do I love about them?
   d. Expanding the theme.
   e. Recognizing help along the way.
   f. Leap of faith.
7. Activity 116

Chapter Twenty Six: Finding God Or The Glass Ceiling...... 117

1. Does Anyone Ever Find God?...117
   a. We must have eyes to see the Presence of God.
2. Universality...117
   a. We develop a god-like mind by using Universal or God Mind.
   b. Seek to understand. Be willing to be misunderstood. You will be different.
3. The Glass Ceiling...118
   a. The choice to stay in three-dimensional thinking.
   b. The rite of passage.
   c. Fear is the separator
4. Finding God 119
   a. Experience of knowing and honoring what comes from other than your own intellect.
   b. From believing to knowing.
   c. Personal attachments to lesser things fall away.
5. Partnership With God..119
   a. We are invited by the fact of our creation

  b. *Self-image is crucial*

6. Being God...120
  a. *Know God is all of you.*
  b. *Being on your purpose always.*
  c. *"Christ in you, your hope of glory."*

7. Not God 121
  a. *Acts of God (according to insurance companies)*
  b. *God is not the manifestation.*

8. God..122
  a. *"I Am That I Am!" No rationale, no qualifiers.*
  b. *Spiritual interpretation brings us to acceptance. Our response to experience heightens into co-creatorship with God.*

9. Miscreations Jettisoned 122

10. Activity 124

Chapter Twenty Seven: Creating The New World 126

1. New World Order...126
  a. *At least someone is talking about it!*
  b. *Clashing of opposites softens into peace talks.*
  c. *The good news is, if we made this mess, we can unmake it.*

2. About Yourself 127
  a. *What is your present state of mind?*
  b. *What stages has your life gone through?*
  c. *What world do you live in now?*
  d. *Your life is your textbook.*

3. Beginning Our New World..128
  a. *The same energy creates failure and success.*
  b. *Reclaim your energy from old emotional habits and redirect it.*
  c. *What would your self-talk be?*

    d. Be aware of what you are feeling at any given moment.
4. Aware And Free To Choose 129
    a. Practice, practice, practice. Start easy.
    b. Your mind is a natural problem solver. Give it something great to work on.
    c. Can't I just ask God to give me a good life and forget all this work? Ultimately, yes, but again it is your mind that blocks God's gifts.
5. Good Is For Us And Everyone 130
    a. We have only scratched the surface of good.
    b. The final frontier. To bring spiritual joy into all life experience.
6. Soaring Over Mountains 130
    a. We just not settle for miniscule good
7. We Are Being Shown 131
    a. We've come a long way, baby, from single cells to godlings.
8. Ask To See 132
    a. Ask to see the more advanced design for being. You can handle it!
    b. When you run dry of ideas, ask God for more.
9. Activity 133

Chapter Twenty Eight: Choosing The Design 134

1. The Silver Screen Of Creation 134
    a. Choices we make in the next dimension.
    b. What I don't want. Sometimes that is the easier place to begin.
2. Let's Try 135
    a. How will you enter the new realm?
    b. How will you communicate?
    c. What about having children?
    d. What about sex?
    e. What about government?
    f. What about God?

3. We innately know where home is. Follow your bliss. 138
   a. *The voice of God.*
   b. *"Why do you weep?"*
   c. *"Where no man has gone before" because it is not the form of man but in the likeness of God that we go there.*
   d. *Divine revelation is the launch pad to create the divine design of your own being.*
   e. *Man, the hand of God, stretching forth through eternity, so God can experience as well as Be.*

Epilogue..141

About the Author 143

Bibliography..145

INTRODUCTION

For several years, I sat down at the computer, feeling a book forming inside of me somewhere. Time and again I had the intention of getting started and gave up after staring at the blank screen for a period of time.

In April of 1994, I visited a kibbutz in Israel. Upon meeting the woman who was the director of the place, I felt this immediate connection with her:

Christine

I found a sister spirit here.
We knew each other well.
Upon first glance and words of truth,
And laughter—joy and laughter!

Into each other's arms we flew!
We were never a world apart.
Although we hail from other lands,
We'll always inhabit one heart.
Author

Note: Over the years I have written poetry when inspired by a particular event in my life, such as meeting Christine. I became aware that many of those lines of poetry would serve a purpose in this book. They are my way of bringing the mystical into the prose of explaining the ideas. I wanted to have a reminder while "learning how" that this is a spiritual endeavor, so readers wouldn't lose sight of the goal while wading through the details. My own poetry will be designated with the word "Author."

I am a minister graduated and ordained in Unity, which is a new thought movement. Our churches teach the power of positive thinking, the metaphysical interpretation of the Bible, and how to use spiritual principle in everyday life. Our world headquarters is located at Unity Village, Missouri.

This deep and beautiful woman asked me the crucial question that started everything: "The Anglican church has an oral tradition. In Unity what is your oral tradition?"

I told her that our oral tradition was to speak spiritual truth into our own lives and to metaphysically interpret the events and experiences of our lives in spiritual terms. We discussed this at length on into the evening. In the Bible book of John 8:32 we find the promise, "you shall know the truth and the truth will make you free." Jesus was speaking of the spiritual truth of your being, which means you are created a spiritual being. You are not a worm of the dust, but a child of God. Speaking spiritual truth is reminding yourself of this. It will be more fully explained throughout the chapters of this book.

The word metaphysical simply means "beyond the physical." The American Heritage Dictionary says: "Investigating the nature of first principles and the problems of ultimate reality ... the study of being ..." Being is referred to as spirituality, that which is non-tangible, of the soul.

Spiritual terms are used to describe our spiritual nature. For instance Truth is used to describe our relationship to our Creator and the spiritual realm, which Jesus mentioned as his kingdom, which was "not of this world." The word "knowing" is another term used indicating stepping into the spiritual which is beyond mere belief. It is taken from the Bible phrase "Be still and know that I am God." The word "know" indicates embodiment, or the engagement of our whole consciousness of thoughts, feelings, and awareness in our relationship to the Creator.

Upon my return home from Israel to San Jose, California, before I even unpacked my suitcases, I sat down at my computer and 12 chapter titles rolled out effortlessly through my fingers, onto the keys, and out-pictured on the screen. Her question was the trigger. The time had come.

WHAT I BELIEVE

I believe that the ultimate tool in spiritual living is to be skilled in interpreting your life according to higher understanding.

I believe that in this higher place, we rise out of all the undesirable perceptions of physical/emotional experience into a joy-filled creative way of being.

I believe our Creator/Sustainer intended our spiritual growth and development, and that we direct our own spiritual evolution.

I believe Jesus saw his lifetime as part of the fabric of becoming God's image, and that everyone was intended to evolve into the likeness of God as well.

I believe we can do what Jesus did, if we will walk daily in a fourth-dimensional or spiritual understanding, seeing the physical realm as the vehicle of spiritual experience.

The spiritual or fourth dimension is the home of miracles as a way of life, which is the Unlimited Divine Potential expressing through us as us. Miracles were natural to Jesus, and so they are to us as well.

At one time in my life when I was a bit frustrated with other people, a dear friend said to me, "You have to remember, Carole, that others walk in the third dimension and occasionally touch the fourth. You walk in the fourth dimension most of the time."

I was really surprised by this statement. The spiritual work I had done up to that time had evidently started demonstrate in my life. From then on I began to pay a lot more attention to who and what I was as someone who walks mostly on the invisible side of the line.

There is still that part of me that very much deals in the three dimensional, physical/emotional side of being. The thuds and jolts of the world are still present in my experience, and perhaps I am a bit more sensitive to them than I think I ought to be! There is nothing wrong with being sensitive, but we shouldn't be irritable.

This is a new world of experience and I feel like an explorer in a new land. I am never quite sure what is beyond the next mountain. This has started me on an expedition into exploring and sharing what I can about the spiritual journey as I know and understand it.

Jesus said, "In the world you will have tribulation ... to the overcomers I will give them to sit in my throne with me ..." Rev. 3:21

There it is, from the Master himself: the three dimensional world, the overcoming, and the fourth dimension, being in that higher place. How do we design the tapestry of our lives with this double thread of experience?

No one comes into our experience by accident or at random. Everyone comes to mirror some part of ourselves so we can see what has not been visible to us. All of our experiences with others may not be easy, but the lesson and the gift of knowledge are always wonderful! Planet Earth is a school and we are here to learn.

My sincere gratitude goes to everyone who has been in my life, especially, those with whom I have had close relationships. We all held the mirror for each other. I finally learned to look into it with love instead of fear. I have learned to see my relationship with God in those mirrors.

Now I hope I can give back another gift, that of being able to see far beyond our individuality into our universality.

I sincerely hope that what I have to share will be of assistance, will be comforting, and will be inspiring to all who seek to find the spiritual pathway for themselves.

How to continue to read this book: I begin by explaining as clearly as possible spiritual interpretation with examples. Spiritual interpretation is a large field that takes thought and practice. The explanations of the many facets of it will continue throughout the chapters. Spiritual interpretation is a very personal endeavor. Ultimately no one can interpret for you, but there are many tools included that will help you receive greater benefit in learning spiritual interpretation and using it in your life.

It is good to digest one chapter at a time. Don't stop with just reading it. We do that with too many books. The activities are intended to help you deepen your experience of the material and make it your own. There are narratives of students who have done the work. They are included to help you get past some of the snags they experienced as they worked on the exercises. They were happy to have their comments printed verbatim so you could get a sense of the classroom experience as well as their insights.

What makes this book unique is its practicality. It brings spiritual practice into the moment and makes it useful to change and enhance your life. Even so, it doesn't lose the mystery. It has the added dimension of creating for yourself what your greater expression of spiritual living might look like. If we are evolving spiritually, and I believe we are, how will things be different? Before his death Jesus said he was going to prepare a place for us. He didn't say much more about it, except to live his spiritual teachings now, and then we would know the way. This book goes on to reach into that new realm, to explore, and to answer the question, "Are we ready to know the way?"

CHAPTER ONE

WHAT IS SPIRITUAL INTERPRETATION?

"… the metaphysician stands in the factory of Mind and sees thoughts poured into visibility …"

Charles Fillmore: <u>Talks On Truth</u>, p. 18-19

I've noticed that the section on spirituality or metaphysics in the bookstores includes the psychic, the karmic, the ghoulish and the strange. It includes past lives, talking to the dead, satanic ritual, and any weird thing folks can think up to experience. Yes, we do ultimately think up our experiences, but that is another chapter.

This book is not about being psychic, karmic or weird. This book is about living now, in a larger world than we now see. It is about being involved in a celestial tapestry of our own choosing and yet of God.

This book is about understanding who, what, and why you are at any given moment. It is about understanding our greater purpose, our higher nature and how it all fits into divine order.

The word metaphysics simply means "beyond the physical." The American Heritage Dictionary says:

"Investigating the nature of first principles and the problems of ultimate reality … the study of being …" That "being" referred to is spirituality, that which is non-tangible, but of the soul.

We have reserved this area for the mystic and the scholar, considering it beyond our comprehension and probably of no earthly use anyway.

Charles Fillmore, co-founder of Unity School of Christianity, and Elizabeth Sand Turner, Unity author, expanded metaphysical interpretation of the Bible into the arena of personal living.

Indeed, the teachings of Unity are ultimately aimed at the spiritual interpretation of one's own life, and the practical every day living of spiritual principle.

WHAT IS REAL AND WHAT ISN'T

Is it reality or fantasy to view our lives from any perspective other than the physical, literal, or historical? The general belief of humanity is this: if you can't tie it, dye it, fry it, or fly it, then it is not real. This is a three-dimensional or physical perspective. This indicates that dreams should be relegated largely to fantasies produced by body chemistry somehow. Hunches and coincidences are thought to be of little importance, and God is only for those who haven't the strength to take personal responsibility.

A young friend of mind slipped into a coma several times during a life threatening illness when she was approximately 12 years old. She had several experiences during these comas that touched her at very deep levels. She said before these experiences happened, she considered this world to be reality, and the world she experienced in her coma to be a fantasy. Throughout the following months, however, that perception began to reverse itself.

What world had she experienced? Life after death? Fantasy produced by body chemistry fighting to maintain life? Wishful thinking? Jesus said, "In my Father's house are many mansions ...," or many dimensions of life experience. Did he know of another dimension about which we should be more aware? Is it the dimension of a larger, more universal experience of life? He seemed to draw the purpose of his ministry and spiritual empowerment from this universal place rather than from earthly sources.

"Life more abundant!" he said. What could that be? Are we not as alive as we will ever be? Yes, but we are not as aware of it as we must be to experience and utilize the full force of being alive. We refer to it as potential, capacity, growth, development, latent or undiscovered power. Colleges and universities are geared toward exploring potential, but mostly at the intellectual levels. "Life more abundant" in this more universal perception, is not usually a classroom subject.

LOOKING FOR THE SPIRITUAL DIMENSION

We are looking for pathways of light where we can walk in confidence. We are seeking a conscious expansion of our ability to co-create with God. We deserve to be in a safe place where joy reigns supreme. We need to be able to see clearly to the heart of everything we experience, and invoke divine wisdom to accompany us each step of the way.

Charles Fillmore, the co-founder of Unity, said that he always went straight to headquarters for his guidance. He was referring to the highest Source known to humankind, God accessed through our Christ nature. We don't need an intercessor or alternate route to God. Jesus told us to go into our "closet", our innermost nature, and speak to our Father in secret. Just God and us. You also don't need to speak in King James thee's and thou's. Plain everyday language from the heart will do. God knows you through and through, and will hear as only God can. Just talk deep inside. Speak clearly about what is happening, how you feel, and what the highest longing of your heart is.

Well, if God knows what we need before we ask, why bother to pray? We need to get ourselves clear in our own thinking and feeling. It is like cleaning a window to let the light shine through. You make of yourself the clearest channel possible for God's life and energy to flow through you. God gives us what we are clear about. If you want the highest and best, your life according to your divine nature, then you need to be as clear as possible in your understanding of what that is. Hopefully, this book will provide some of the framework and ideas you can use to bring that clarity to your thinking and spiritual practice.

WHAT IS SPIRITUAL INTERPRETATION?

This is a tool, a ladder, a way of being. As a tool it turns the nuts and bolts that create a new structure into being. For instance, I may think my boss is irritated with me today:

- Practically we can say, maybe it isn't me at all, but something that happened to him or her at home.
- Psychologically we can say that we both need to work on our stuff.
- Spiritually or metaphysically we can say that we are co-creating a new way of existing together, finding our godlikeness, by being mirrors to each other.

Spiritually we are one, made of the same God stuff, moving together on an eternal journey of unfolding divinity.

We are learning to transform the world by beginning with ourselves, and this is a marvelous learning experience.

As a ladder, spiritual interpretation lifts us up to a higher perception of what is happening to us and to the world around us. The higher we go in consciousness, the more we can see. A greater picture comes into view and tells us a greater story about life. It lifts our conscious thinking to a greater awareness of our spiritual potential so that life energy is quickened in us. "Life more abundant." We know the quickening effect of a good fright, where the adrenaline is increased, our awareness is sharper, and our whole physical and mental demeanor is on alert.

This also happens at the spiritual level. The quicker the vibration of our spiritual awareness, the keener we are in mind and body without the tension of fear. We can begin to get a sense of what it is to be in our higher nature, our spiritual nature.

This higher nature is alluded to in 2Corinthians 5:16. "From now on we regard no one from a human point of view; even though we once regarded Christ from a human point of view, we regard him thus no longer. Therefore if anyone is in Christ, he is a new creation; the old has passed away; behold, the new has come."

As we experience a new way of being, or become a "new being as Christ" awareness, we learn to live from our Christ nature. We find ourselves shifted in some wonderful way, and we function differently inside and out. For instance, our thinking begins to change in terms of hopefulness, compassion, and a sense of coming from a greater perspective as we regard any situation. Peace begins to unfold within us that surpasses human understanding.

The writer of the book of Revelation calls it "going into the courts of the Lord and going no more out." We find we have moved slowly and gently over a threshold. It is like growing up. It is written in Ephesians 4:15, "We are to grow up in every way ... into Christ."

We suddenly look back upon our lives and find that "we've come a long way, baby!" You are different from the you of five years ago (or even five months ago). In Christ you are wise, light hearted, fearless, aware of choices at every juncture, centered in spirit, and empowered to do good for all concerned.

We do not become exempt from earthly events, but we can choose our response to them. We no longer need to become panicked in an emergency. We know a higher way of dealing with it now. We are aware of all levels at once and function simultaneously on them all. What are those levels?

- The physical emergency, which we meet at the physical level. We stop the bleeding and bandage the wound.
- The emotional and psychological ramifications are clear to us. A traumatized person will need counseling, support and care.
- Spiritual perfection, not physical appearance, is reality, and we are safe even though the surrounding appearances seem threatening.

We are able to give first aid, encouragement, and pray simultaneously. We are multilevel beings. The emergency is like a quiz or test. It is our opportunity to give the most universal and complete response we can muster at that moment. This is our opportunity to see how well we have learned our lessons in godlikeness. This is our chance to see where we can improve (where we panicked), and work on it.

WHERE ARE WE GOING WITH THIS?

In the book of Revelation it is written, "To the overcomers I will grant you to sit with me on my throne beside me, as I myself conquered and sat down with my Father on His throne." Rev. 3:21

We become aware of our part as a co-creative, seemingly peer relationship with God through our Christ nature, just as Jesus was. We become spiritually empowered to do the greater things. We begin living in the Kingdom as a godlike being. In this way we become true heirs to the Kingdom of Absolute Good.

Spiritual interpretation is beautiful, always positive and helpful. The help is in the area of the soul. Percy Bysshe Shelly wrote:

> A poet is a nightingale,
> Who sits in darkness and sings
> To cheer its own solitude with sweet sounds.
> His auditors are as men entranced
> By the melody of an unseen musician,
> Who feel that they are moved and softened,
> Yet know not whence or why.

In being moved and softened, our lives are lovelier in ways we can hardly describe. Our prayers become prayers of thanks breathed quietly in the privacy of our own perception of the divine.

We misuse spirituality when we use what we learn to blame ourselves or someone else for our circumstances. It is misuse when we accuse ourselves or someone else of not being spiritual because illness or misfortune happened. These teachings are to be used for our upliftment only. We are to focus upon how we can change from here on, not whether we think we goofed up in the past.

We spiritually interpret because we are spirit indwelling a physical body, producing a lifetime. We interpret because we are the curiosity of God discovering who We are. We interpret because we are on this planet, not of it. We are created. Only the body is born. We are far more than our finite intellectual mind can comprehend. There are dimensions to us that we have not yet discovered. Just as a child has not yet experienced adolescence, adults find more potential as they mature not only in years, but in mind. The wealthy industrialist suddenly asks him or herself, is that all there is? The minister or priest will suddenly feel as if they are losing their faith. It is because we have come to the end of one dimension of thinking and are on the threshold of the next. Discovering our spirituality is another dimension. Discovering ways to live it is another. We are great multidimensional beings focusing upon a short lifetime of earthly experiences with eternal impressions.

> We began
> Somewhere in the glow of a celestial ocean;
> Waves of our being
> Touching so many distant shores,
> And then suddenly touching each other,
> Like silver threads being drawn
> Through an intricate pattern ...
> Smoothly, harmoniously, perfectly
> By a loving Creator
> Who did not begin,
> But Is.
>
>   Author

CHAPTER TWO

WHAT IS IN A LIFETIME?

As children we tend to believe that events just happen day to day, and we have little control over them or over the direction of our lives. Our parents, family members, teachers, and caregivers were the major influences shaping the events we experienced. For instance if we were constantly told that there wasn't enough money, food, or things to go around, we responded to events according to the scarcity we have been trained to believe in. If we were constantly taught that we were sinners, unworthy of good, then we lived our lives feeling we were guilty of something terrible and, as a result, we were worthless.

When we grow out of childhood and become capable of thinking for ourselves, we often don't change from our childhood attitudes and continue to live out these early impressions. One way to change this is to neutralize the impact of these early years. Two things will help us do that. One is to realize that the people involved were doing the best they knew, and if they knew better, they would have done better. The second is to look back applying a spiritual understanding and finding the gifts of learning from those experiences that will benefit us now and in the future.

It may be hard to believe that people who mistreated us in childhood didn't know better. Those who mistreat and abuse others almost invariably come from a long line of abusers. They were abused and their parents who abused them were abused. It has taken humanity many generations to learn this. One of the first books I read that spoke to this was written by Dorothy C. Briggs, entitled "Your Child's Self Esteem." As I read it, my own eyes were opened wide to the hurtful attitudes and behaviors I had learned and carried on into my adult life. It was difficult at first to understand that I was doing only what I knew, and now I could do better. Self forgiveness and forgiveness of others is the first step, but just saying "I forgive" isn't quite enough. It has to be under girded with understanding that enables us to release the hurt.

The second step, spiritually interpreting what happened in the past, enables you to get the gift that has been waiting for you. Spiritual interpretation means that we rise above the event and its physical/psychological ramifications, and ask "What good can I learn?" You have never deserved abuse or ill treatment of any kind. So the lesson is not to be found in deserving punishment, but in the realm of finding strength and compassion for yourself and others. It is essential to apply the compassion to yourself first. We must heal ourselves first and then we can reach out to others.

In order to have material to practice forgiveness and spiritual interpretation, sketch out in a notebook the story of your life. This will take some time. Give it the hours, days, or weeks that it might require. Hopefully, it won't take too long, but it is important to get some of it on paper.

The first reason to write your life story is to be able to examine it in a new light. The second reason is to be able to make peace with it and release it. When we are not at peace and hang on to old hurts, we tend to create our future out of the same thing. Being able to bless it and let it go eventually frees you to create a future that is not a rubber stamp of the past, but new, alive, and exciting.

Writing your life story can be filled with emotional snags that you will want to get past. To help you deal with these, twenty-two wonderful people volunteered their time and energy to go through this experience. They gave me permission to share with you their words about what it was like for them to write their story. They experienced some rewards and wanted you to be successful along with them in receiving the gift contained in doing the work. Here are some excerpts from their conversations written exactly as they expressed them. Their names are designated by the first letter only to preserve their privacy:

> J. One of the things I was experiencing as I wrote my life story was that I got a feeling as if someone were looking over my shoulder. It was a feeling of a little disappointment that there wasn't something more exciting that I could write about ... I shared that with my son and he said, "That's probably your view!" I've done some of this writing before and went through a lot of problems, but this time I could see it from a higher perspective. More like, it just is what it is without my projecting.

> L. I had done this before in a religious setting. As I'm working on this, I notice that this time, hopefully, it's a little more spiritual than in previous times. Before, I was really interested in putting down all my accomplishments and just kind of stroking myself. This is a lot different.

> A. This has been very interesting for me. I'm surprised at the detail I'm putting into my story. I was thinking of my first memory. It's different than just

digging into problems. It's just my story, and the people who came to mind are relatives, friends and occasions. I'm enjoying it. It is really exciting!

C. I was really having a hard time getting started with it, until I read the suggestion to split it up into decades. I was amazed at how vividly I recalled my first memory. I could feel the wind in my hair at age two! I've been journaling on a daily basis for more than seven years and I was amazed at the things that came up when I just opened my mind and let Spirit flow!

B. I think I am very analytical. I don't just like the facts, so when I think of a memory, I think of the age I was and the problem I was working on then.

S. In the past I had done a chart called a lifeline, where I actually draw a graph and layout with little pictures. What I find coming up for me is an overarching theme of this life. One of those themes is how I am gifted with talents, intelligence, and creativity, and how that was encouraged or blocked, and how I internalized that.

Author: It might help to stick with facts and not get lost in impacts. Impacts and reactions cause you to get stuck in the psychological level. That can be like a squirrel cage wheel. We go around and around. I want to help us move out of psychology into spirituality.

A. I had sheets of paper for every five years with categories so that I had a place to write everything so I didn't get lost. It helped me keep my focus. It really helped me to hear that we don't have to relive it.

D. It's done. I'm glad it's done, but it wasn't fun. It was like putting it on a TV screen and watching it. I've done that a thousand times and I don't want to do it again.

Author: This is good information. It gives other people who may not be able to enjoy writing their life story permission to honor their real feelings about it. It is O.K. not to enjoy it.

D. Another thing that helped was that you gave us permission not to censor ourselves.

Author: It takes some courage not to censor as you write. It really does. It is great that you were willing to go for it!

V. I was kind of bored with it. I mean I don't think it is boring. I think it is interesting material, but I'm just personally bored with it.

Author: That's good! I say this because in order to move on into a cosmic story, moving into another level, you have to be able to let this level go. We will stop the writing and deal with our history shortly, and onto the next step. You have been in my classes for several years, and I am sure you are ready to make that shift.

L. Mine was like writing about some other life. One thing I really enjoyed about it was my childhood years. I forgot all the accomplishments and things that really made me feel happy. Mine was not like a story. I was more just jumping into things … a lot of negative things, like marriages that didn't work … so, I was regrouping, remembering things that were good. It gave me a lot to think about.

L. I was delving more into my feelings about why I was so frightened about life as a small child. What prompted me to hide from people? I realized that there is a part of me that is still very shy. I had no idea that was still living in me.

K. I want to go to the next step. I want to interpret it. I want to know what this means! There was a point in my life when any of the things I would have written down, Oh man! I would have relived it. This made it a lot safer, to just write it down as a story rather than relive it!

B. I think this helped me put a lot of pieces together. I don't feel so sectioned off in pieces and parts. I was afraid it would bog me down and make my life today a little more difficult because of dealing with issues that were not resolved. Now I feel like I'm writing and it is not having that effect on me.

S. My life seems like a series of chaotic periods, and when I got a handle on it, it became easier to write about. But when things happen in my life that I don't understand, then I find difficulty writing about them.

D. When I look at major events it depresses me. So I need to look at my daily activities.

Author: Was it a good experience to write your life story?

D. No. I didn't do it. I got to page 23 and stopped.

Author: Do you have more recent things you can write about that are not so painful, so you have something to work with? I encourage all of you to write about the last six months especially. Skip over early things and fill them in later if you are running out of time.

> J. This time I'm writing my life story from a spiritual sense. Writing about what got me to this place from wherever I came from. I can't do chronological. Chronological order does not work for me. I'm writing on four levels at the same time.

> S. I'm amazed how vivid some of these memories are today and the pain is still very great. I have to look at it.

Author: As one participant related, his life story was too painful to write, so he concentrated on his daily activities and just doing a good job each present moment.

If your story is far to painful, pick out a few positive events to describe, or just write about the recent past. In fact, you can start with the most recent events and move back in time until you get to the place where you feel you need to stop and simply turn the rest over to God.

As you write your story, be gentle with yourself! Be sure to focus more on recent stuff than struggling with remembering details of your early childhood. Once you learn to spiritually interpret a few life experiences, you will see your whole life in a new light. You will eagerly anticipate future events and they will be more exciting and meaningful.

Here are some suggestions to help you begin:

a. What have you been told about your early life?

Sometimes it is hard to sort out what you have been told from what you actually remember. Put it all in, but distinguish as best you can.

b. What are your most vivid memories, positive or negative?

c. Which memories posted a significant change or turning point in your life, for better or worse? Use a highlighter to mark them all.

d. What are the significant events in your life within the past year?

e. A family photograph album might be helpful, and/or making an outline of each decade and filling it in.

Double space your history and leave large margins so you can make notes. This is the beginning of the journal of the spiritual interpretation of your life.

You may begin to sense a pattern or a path. A larger picture may be emerging. This is good, but don't be concerned with it at this point. Don't try to manufacture fanciful connections or synchronicities. Just let the history flow.

If you get bogged down emotionally on a scene, just make an outline of it. You can fill in details later if you choose to use the story for an interpretation. Try to be as neutral as possible, as though you were a distant observer of the event. This may be difficult at first, but the more objective you can be, the more clearly the interpretation will appear later on.

Keep your history journal in a private place and don't share it with others. The thought of others seeing it and judging it will be inhibiting. You will tend to delete what others might not approve of or agree with you about.

Most of all, do this in a prayerful state of mind. Remember that all is known in the celestial realms and is not judged. Even your blackest moments are seen through the most loving eyes that you can imagine.

Here are some quick reference points to get you started:
BEGIN TO FRAME IT WITH:
1. Earliest memories, childhood experiences and feelings
2. What events got me to where I am today? In my career, my awareness?
3. Who were the significant people along the way? Why?

BE SURE TO INCLUDE SIGNIFICANT DETAILS:
1. What are the high points of my life experience?
2. What are the low points?
3. What are my most significant events?
4. What are significant turning points?

CONCLUDE WITH THE PRESENT DAY:
1. What has happened in this past year?
2. How do I see my life progressing?

Sketch the story out as best you can. Details will come to you as you let your mind know what you want. You can always add more later on. Don't judge.

CHAPTER THREE

GETTING TO THE BLESSING

"… the human condition is a blessed one. It is a mirror, a faithful replica of the spirit's situation."

Emmanuel's Book p.4

How is it that the human condition is a blessed one? As we look out over the world, we see that blessings seem to be unevenly distributed. We look at the challenge, and often the pain, of writing our own life story, and see that it wasn't all blessing, at least not according to our human definition. For some of my students, writing their life story was impossible, because it was so painful they had to block it out just to go on living. When the human psyche is so traumatized that it has to go into survival mode, how can Emmanuel call it blessed?

The fact that these people are surviving at whatever level of conscious awareness they have, says that they are creating a new story. They are weaving as best they can the fabric of a life so it can go on. My God, my God, you have not forsaken me after all, but have given me a life raft so that I can still reach my destination. Blessing! And here begins the blessing of spiritual interpretation.

WHY AND HOW TO SPIRITUALLY INTERPRET YOUR LIFE!

Aha! The big question "why" begs a rationale, and this is exactly what you must have to satisfy the intellectual mind. The intellect deserves satisfaction at certain levels, because it struggles to help you make sense of your life. A rationale is a story you tell your mind about why and how an event fits into your life. It is a personal philosophy that, hopefully, helps you handle events in a constructive way for your greatest good.

The intellect is a tool, a work area, a knowledge sorter, but it is not an instrument of wisdom. The intellect is part of the psychological nature. Wisdom is an aspect of the spiritual.

We often try to make the intellect wise. When making a decision, we list pros and cons, trying to decide on the logical basis of weight and balance. After we've written this all out, made lists, looked at all sides of an issue, we often still can't decide. To make matters worse, the pros and cons of today often switch places tomorrow. We then make a decision contrary to all logical indications. How confusing and baffling unless, of course, you understand that wisdom from spirit will quietly slip in and point the way through the confusion.

So what do you need for a rationale? What story do you need to tell yourself about how you came to occupy your body, be in your particular family, in this century, helping the world to do what it must do? Somewhere, somehow, did you choose it? If so, what part of you chose it and when? What was the criteria? Were you merely an accident of nature? Was there a plan or was it just happenstance?

I have a story I like to tell my self and you are welcome to use my it, create your own, or incorporate someone else's ideas. After all, we are all on the same team, aren't we?

We were all beings in spiritual bodies in Cosmic Forces Class together before we began to be born. We had to have a class project, so we decided to inhabit a planet in physical form and learn to be creative in the dense vibration called physicality.

This would be no small undertaking! Physicality was more dense and confusing that we counted on, and we began to get lost in it. While playing in the pleasures of physical sensation and beauty, we began staying too long until we forgot who we were originally and why we came.

We began to think that we were first physical beings, a whole new erroneous identity. We believed that physical things were the only reality. We thought of ourselves as lowly clods made of dust, and that pain was our punishment for something we must have done wrong. We began to criticize ourselves and make up wrongs that we must surely have committed. We even made our very birth wrong and called it "original sin."

In our error thinking we made ourselves sick, we aged and became disabled, or we had injurious accidents. These things eventually caused us to die in the physical. Only after the death of the body did we remember who we were.

We became so stuck in this slow physical vibration that the captain of our project had to come into physical form to wake us up before we lost the whole project and flunked the class! His Earth name was Jesus or Yeshua. We treated him rather badly because we were so lost and scared that we didn't recognize him. But he did get the job done despite our density. He did replant the seed of spiritual awareness in us. It took root in the disciples and other followers of "The Way" and began to slowly spread from person to person, re-germinating in the consciousness.

Thankfully, we are now beginning to awaken to our spiritual nature again and to understand who and what we are. It has been a long slow process for almost two thousand years, but it is happening more quickly now. The more of us that can awaken, the less power physicality has over all of humankind and the sooner we will all completely awaken together. We will all be changed "In the twinkling of an eye." So we are all trying to open those spiritual eyes and get them twinkling together. Once awake we can begin work as co-creators with God, our true vocation.

Back to my class, once again my twenty-two researchers met with me to discuss their experience in working with this chapter. Unlike writing their life stories, this was uncharted territory. We were asking the big questions about life, and they were concerned that they couldn't write a cosmic story because they didn't have answers.

L. When I was about six years old I really pondered, "If God created Heaven and Earth, then who created God?" My mother told me to just give it up. But I really thought about where I came from and where I am going. I'm not sure I believe in reincarnation.

Author: We need to get into a story-telling mode. Who knows if there was ever a Cosmic Forces class? It was just a way of explaining something. The story of Adam and Eve was an imaginative story to explain the beginning of things, not to be taken as historical fact. Since we teach that we are all one in spirit, then it stands to reason that we must have all been together before we got here. That's why I came up with Cosmic Forces class. I envisioned us all sitting around a large shining table because two friends of mine had had that dream on the same night in different parts of the country. It makes sense that this planetary existence is an ongoing project because we all keep coming to work on it and then leaving through dying. A bit of fantasy helps move the story along, just as stories like Jason and the Golden Fleece are fantasy, but reveal a spiritual journey to us.

V. I mentioned last week that I was getting bored with my life story, but this was fun. I went to the beach and ran out of ink. I sort of wrote like a child's story. In the beginning when there was only knowledge, the universe was full of intelligence and the intelligence was with God and was God, and the intelligence became aware of himself and He began to look about and began to experience inner aspects of himself. And God spoke within his intelligence and asked the question … and I stepped forward and was born of the spirit.

The spirit was full of perfect love, in perfect union and perfect peace and we dwell with God and God is our father and mother and we live in her womb and in his belly in a place called heaven. And there is ageless beauty for there is no time, no death or decay. And in heaven every living creature has a voice, and everything could speak, the flowers, trees and animals. The wind would carry the song of all the living creatures singing in unison, "Glory, glory, glory Great God Almighty."

And there was a sound that permeated the universe in music far more beautiful that human ears have heard and we danced with each other in a great sea of clouds while the stars and the animals too, kept time and praised God. In heaven there was no such thing as separation. The glory of God was intelligence and the joy of God's creation, and God spoke once again to his creation and asked the question, "Who am I and who would like to be expanded? And I came forward ...

When I said the glory of God was intelligence and the joy of God's creation, that is how it feels to me, like God just wants to know, experience. And so it seems like it is the nature of God to explore.

Author: How does the concept of war fit into "God exploring?"

V. Pulling things apart so we can look at it.

Author: What is the relative condition of the world?

V. There's more light than darkness I think. There's a lot of stuff that we are not real happy about, a lot of bad things, but humanity doesn't seem to know who they are.

I guess because I've been through a serious period of depression, I've been going through this period of trying to reconnect with God. I feel like there's been a complete separation for a very long time. I knew there was something for me, but I could not figure out what that was, so now I'm trying to reconnect what happened. Why did I feel so bad for so long ... swimming upstream and trying to get back. Not even fully knowing what I'm going to get out of it but just having a strong desire to get there, trying to find the light, trying to have a good family and it brought me to the stage of reading Job again.

I'm struggling. There's a lot of darkness for me. I'm swimming in darkness seeking love.

Author: Can you see the planet struggling towards the light?

V. I'm exhausted by it. I read all night long. I pray and meditate. For some reason the light came on. Keep swimming. Every stroke I take something new happens.

C. I struggled with an idea because last week it dawned on me that I have so much in me that mankind or any individual or I can only go so high. We don't have the ability to go higher in the intellect. I'm struggling with that. My cosmic story is kind of like there is everything. And mankind struggles to get to that end. And the more we try different ways of getting there, I keep coming back to the idea that I don't have to struggle, but I do have to expand or I don't get anywhere.

Don't you think that all these experiences we have all the time through our lives, from childhood to adulthood or whatever stage, all these experiences and unfortunately some of them are bad experiences ... every time, you learn from that?

If you can look at it in a way that turns it around, every bad thing, every good thing, that the more things you experience, the more you move up and up. I did that, I got through it. I made it! I survived and I am here now. You'll be over in that place for a while and something else will come up. It's really tough. But you look and see that it will pass. It's all an accelerating process, moving on and on with God, and all these experiences are part of it.

Some opportunity is going to come along for others. Maybe they need to work through poverty, or something different. They can make the best of it or make the worst of it. We're all at different places learning different things because there are so many of us!

Author: We can begin to think about meaning. What is our relationship to God? What is our value on the planet, and what is our purpose? This is a big consideration for me now. I think about it constantly. What am I really? How will my evolution be affected by recognizing that we are going through a serious evolution as individuals and people, but we first have to look at it individually. How do we move on to the next step?

I am hearing from all of you that you are looking at these difficult and painful experiences and saying that they are a part of you. Yes, it is O.K. to dwell here for a while, but it feels like going downward. And you see that it is a choice and that is where the power is. The feelings are your choice.

So start looking at the cosmic picture of the condition of humanity. What is the goal of humanity? What is our goal? What are we reaching for? Where are we going?

When we externalize, we judge. When we internalize, we must drop the judgment. Humanity has trapped itself in judgment and maybe it is most often not aware that it judges and that judgment is hurtful. We forget that we are here to explore as V. said, and just taste the joy of being.

L. When I started doing my cosmic story, I didn't start writing. I went into a thirty-minute meditation and I had my tape recorder on. After I came out of the meditation I started talking. My voice was very high and very childlike when I was talking about where I thought I had come from. And slowly as I talked myself through my story, my voice started getting lower and lower, and then I went into almost a rap poem about the condition of humanity. It was real tough, hard, and forceful. I could feel my emotions coming up and my anger coming up, and I felt all these horrible things, and then I had to stop at thinking about the great depression, because I was coming into rage. I had to calm down, get back to meditation. So that's where I am with my cosmic story. I am enraged right now.

Author: How will rage serve humanity?

L. Those are pretty extreme responses to the world, to strike out in anger, rage, and eventually we find that it is not what we want exactly. So humanity has the capacity to stop itself and make a choice.

A. When my story decided to come through was 2:30 a.m. on Monday morning. (laughter) This is what came out: Our assignment is to get to know God better. How we do that is pretty much our choice. It's like going to a travel agent and looking at the endless possibilities of places to go and things to do once we get there. It is up to us to choose our route and live in our life lesson. Some of our choices turn out to be more enjoyable than others. Distant lands can be packed with adventures and fun, and others downright scary. Sometimes we get so far away from home that we forget where we came from. We forget our mission. We forget that we are spiritual beings living in a physical body, or that life lines are always there if we don't do something to keep the help away, or we don't see it and forget where to turn. We need companionship of each other, knowing deep within that we have met once again to guide and support each other. To give loving reminders of what our adventures are all about. Others may not seem so friendly and supportive, but they are nevertheless a jog to our memory. Sometimes we spend more time with a group because the fog gets so thick we can't see through it. As a result we wander around in circles and we forget that we have guidance. (laughter) Then something happens that gives us a glimpse of what we really are about. God is very patient and is willing to wait for us to make the choice. He/She will be right there anytime we are ready to get quiet and listen to that still, small voice within. We don't have to worry about not having another opportunity to find our way because we have forever if that's what it takes to know a wonderful God. I felt good about that and I could go back to sleep!

Reaching back into your life story, what can you find that gave you strength? Was there an event that told you there is something more to you than just physical life? Was there a goodness in you that kept urging you to express it somehow? Was there someone you considered to be a hero you wanted to be like? If there was someone you wanted to be like, what were the qualities they expressed that inspired you? Whether the events were painful or joyful, the gift is always there awaiting your recognition of it. Spiritual interpretation is finding the presence of the Creator and your connection to it, your spirituality. We have been taught we are separate from God. God is "up there" and we are "down here." I believe God is "in here" within us as us. We are not all of what God is, but God is all of what we are. We are separated from God only when we believe we are, but we can never be separated from God in spiritually.

CHAPTER FOUR

FINDING GOD'S THREADS

As we experience life we are creating a huge tapestry that tells the story of our life. It has patterns, symbols, and images that lead us into seeing a larger picture filled with possibilities. You may be able to pick out these patterns and images from the life story you wrote to begin the interpretation of your experiences. Were there things that happened over and over? Did you have a picture in your imagination that seemed significant to your development. Perhaps it will all become clearer as we discuss the twelve essential spiritual threads. We must create a new tapestry because we have been living according to our past and it's stories, and these will not serve us in the greater more expanded life that God created us to live.

We were created in "the image and likeness of God," woven out of the perfect image in God Mind. The Bible says that "God knit us together" in our mother's womb. While our bodies were being formed, God knit our conscious being together after a Godly image. God has given us all the thread we need to continue expanding.

Our spiritual tapestry is woven out of twelve individual threads. We can more effectively weave our tapestry if we know something about the threads God has given us. Tapestry weavers know all about the threads they are using. Threads must be strong and enduring, otherwise the tapestry will not last. The thread must be impervious to rot and decay, beautiful to the eye, and pleasing to the touch.

The weaver knows just how to choose and blend these threads in order to make patterns and not chaos. A thread is chosen with the whole pattern in mind. The weaver holds a larger picture in mind while working with a single thread. The weaver may sketch a pattern on paper as a guide when decisions about threads must be made.

You may feel a bit handicapped because the details are not very clear to you yet. Handicaps can be a blessing if you will consider them as such. They will set your creative impulses free from experiences of the past. Beethoven went completely deaf, but he heard his symphonies from within and conducted them with gusto. Mozart heard the whole *Messiah* in his mind before he began to write the music down. It is reported that even the author of the Harry Potter series saw the whole story from beginning to end before she began to write the first book.

Whether you can see your new life plan or not, you can begin if you have a pattern, a sketch, or simply know the function and capacity of the threads you will use. There is a world of difference between leading a life that has no plan or vision, as we have done in the past, and stepping into the story of our own creation knowing where it is going.

You are going to learn about your threads. If the weaver started with one thread and guessed at the second the result would be chaos. No beautiful pattern could result. No clear goal or vision could be reached.

Charles Fillmore, Co-Founder of Unity, researched those qualities or powers without which human life could not continue. You can find this work in his book, *The Twelve Powers of Man*, published by Unity School of Christianity. For instance, without imagination we could not move across a room because we must imagine something that draws us into movement. Our world would be totally flat without imagination.

Some things he considered were really just part of a greater idea. For instance affection and compassion are part of love. Love would be the power that we could not live without because love is said to be the cosmic glue that draws and holds everything together. So whether or not you have affection, a greater power called love still holds your world together. This is not human love, but the great archetype, the universal pattern of love behind all aspects of love.

Just as one thread cannot make a tapestry, so one power cannot stand alone in a human life. Twelve is "a complete number in relation to the conditions of the manifest." (Dictionary of All Myths and Scriptures) Hence there were not just one, but twelve disciples, twelve tribes, twelve divisions of the zodiac, and many more significant references to the number twelve in the Bible.

The next twelve chapters will be about the twelve essential threads needed for our lives. Charles Fillmore called them the twelve powers of man. He related them to nerve centers in the body that correspond to metaphysical power centers in our consciousness. These power centers, when spiritualized, come under the direction of our Christ or divine nature and work together to manifest the Kingdom of God within us and in our lives.

Charles Fillmore's choices of twelve powers are the threads that will be strong, incorruptible, beautiful and completely comfortable to the touch of mind and soul. You will undoubtedly find many shades of each one that you will want to incorporate according to your individual path, but it is important to know the archetypal ones that are your true foundation.

We call each of our twelve powers into the service of our spiritual nature. Each power within us must be carefully trained and guided until all are spiritually aligned. Each power has a different job to do and requires special handling. Getting to know your powers individually will make your work in life so much easier.

The powers are to be called in a particular order, in the order that Jesus called his disciples. This order had spiritual significance as a pattern for building our spiritual lives. So we will use that same order and relate each thread to the meaning of the corresponding disciple. For instance, faith is represented by the disciple Peter, who was called into service first. This is the first power called because one must have faith that something can happen before any action can be undertaken. If you are aware of this, you will begin your projects with the faith that they will come to fruition.

You will then call upon strength (Andrew) and wisdom (James). You must have strength to begin the action and the wisdom to know what action to take. Love is the fourth power to be called, represented by the disciple John. As mentioned already, love is called the cosmic glue because it holds everything together. Often people start out by summoning the power of love, not realizing that love must have a foundation or it cannot be effective.

Some people start with imagination, represented by Bartholomew, which should be the sixth power called, not the first. Imagination needs the first five powers in place before it is called, or it produces daydreams that will amount to nothing. This is why so many people are disappointed that their dreams do not come true. A little knowledge of the threads needed and how to begin creating the pattern would have made all the difference.

CHAPTER FIVE

FAITH

Without the faith that something can happen we will not begin anything. People who have no faith in themselves will decline to attempt anything beyond their daily routine. We often don't know we have the power of faith until a difficult event renders us devoid of our usual coping devices and safety nets.

Faith seems to come from nowhere to turn circumstances around. But faith is an inherent capacity within us, placed there from the beginning. We can't manufacture it. No one can instill it in us. We must find it wholly within ourselves. The human problem is that we don't discover it and cultivate it. We wait until there is a crisis and it catches us as we fall. Faith is thought to be temporary, until our luck changes. We must awaken to the realization that it is an ongoing power in our lives. Why else would the Creator place it within us?

To stir up the capacity of faith, we need to decide to have faith and to be faithful. The disciple Peter, who represents faith, discovered that it took practice. He stumbled time and again. When he stepped out of the boat on the Sea of Galilee, he momentarily lost his resolve when he saw how high the waves were. When he began to sink he called out to Jesus to save him. Jesus reached out to Peter, lifted him up, and said, "Why did you doubt?" Choosing doubt instead of faith happens because doubt is born of fear and always close at hand.

Peter stumbled again when three times he denied knowing Jesus, even after vowing to go to the death with him. Jesus had been taken to Pilate for trial and all of the disciples were in danger as his followers. An old hag tending a fire in the chill evening beside the city wall recognized Peter and accused him of being Jesus' follower so that all around could hear. Again, in the face of great danger, Peter was afraid and slipped quickly into denial.

You may have to remake your decision for faith many times before you learn to keep hold of that thread as you pull it through your life experiences. Eventually Peter became the most powerful of the disciples, but he had to persevere until the quality of his decision was constant and unfailing. The quality of your decision to rely upon faith is the foundation of your spiritual unfolding. It is the foundation as you work with all the other threads.

The thread may slip from your grasp at the news of the life threatening illness striking a loved one. You may feel it slipping away in the shaking of your knees as you ask for that well-deserved raise in pay. Some things you attempt that seem very simple might fail because you didn't think it necessary to evoke the power of faith.

If something is not manifesting in your life as you would like it to, trace your thread of faith and see if it has broken. If it has, pick up the strands prayerfully and mend them together again.

Faith is the starting place of everything you create in your life. The rescuing kind of faith is called blind faith. But we don't have to wait for disaster to strike in order to experience faith. Thinking faith is when we don't wait for disaster to happen, but consciously create our good outcomes. Thinking faith is when we put faith into the beginning of our plans for our lives. We are aware of it in everything that we do and call it purposefully to be the foundation of our efforts.

Make the decision to strengthen your hold on the power of faith. Eventually the power of faith becomes so much a conscious part of you that it doesn't keep slipping away. It is becomes so securely woven into your tapestry that the thread is evident in every part of the pattern. Treasure and give thanks for its power to support any dream you may have in your heart.

CHAPTER SIX

STRENGTH

Just as faith is an intangible, so we are speaking about the kind of strength that is something other than just our physical and moral fiber. The disciple, Andrew, represents the power of strength. His name in Greek translation means "strong man." True strength is not of the physical or emotional, but of the Spiritual. Our physical strength has very definite limits and when it is exhausted we become weak. If we tax our physical strength without rest, it breaks down the cells of our bodies, making us vulnerable to disease and death.

Our emotional strength is tied to our physical strength and has its limits as well. When emotional strength breaks down, it diminishes physical strength and again the body suffers. When people suffer extreme tortures and maintain their inner strength, we find that it is supported by spiritual strength. Spiritual strength cannot be broken and does not deteriorate the body. Actually spiritual strength maintains the physical body far beyond it's own capacity to survive adverse conditions.

A friend demonstrated the difference with a Popsickle stick and a nail. The stick represented our physical nature and the nail, God. When pressure was put on the Popsickle stick, it broke immediately. When the stick was bound to the metal nail and pressure applied, it could not be broken. When we are consciously one with the spiritual strength, we cannot be broken.

Jesus' spiritual strength carried him far beyond normal physical endurance. He went into the desert regions for long periods of time to fast and pray. There was no indication that he took supplies with him. He took no animal to ride or tent to shelter him. The hills and mountains of Judea are completely barren of vegetation and water. The rocky surfaces are of broken shale and loose gravel, making footholds treacherous and traveling arduous.

On occasion, after ministering to the crowds, his disciples would offer him food, and he would refuse it saying that he had "sustenance they knew not of." There are many books written about spiritual masters who could sustain themselves for long periods of time without food. Some even achieved a catatonic state for extensive periods where they seemed dead. When they revived themselves they were energized and vigorous. These feats are accomplished only by those who, after many years of rigorous training, have achieved a high state of spiritual discipline. This is not for the spiritual novice to attempt.

It is interesting how quickly faith leads to strength as its ally. Praying for strength to keep our decision of faith intact is necessary. Faith and strength need each other and here, early on, we begin to see the barest glimmerings of the design unfold.

There is only one way to tap into our spiritual strength and that is through concentration, contemplation, prayer and/or meditation. This is a thread that we cannot pull through the design without prayer. We have many difficulties in human life that would cause us to believe in weakness. When we pray it is important to affirm our spiritual strength in God. Often people beg God for strength, as if God had not already placed that capacity within them.

Begging conjures up a doubtful state of mind that weakens us and defeats our purpose in praying. "Ask and ye shall receive" is the promise. If you look up the word "ask" in the dictionary, you will find that it does not mean beg. It means "to lay claim to." In praying we lay claim to the spiritual strength God has placed within us and give thanks for this gift. Prayer spiritualizes and enhances our physical and emotional strength, and we will not be broken.

CHAPTER SEVEN

WISDOM

Ah, wisdom ... that golden scepter that is held by a hallowed few: The oracles, the philosophers, the avatars, and saints of long ago. Truly few have availed themselves of the power of wisdom because they don't think it is within each and every one of us. And yet if one can be wise, then we all can be wise, if we know where wisdom lives.

How we dread to be thought a fool! In fact we so dread it, that we will not risk trying to appear wise unless we become drunk on the ego's bluster. Do you know someone who led you on in the pretense that they were wiser than you? And perhaps the results were disastrous when you discovered their deception. If you were led into trouble of some kind, you surely lost your trust in them and perhaps had difficulty in trusting others from then on.

One of the most complete writings on wisdom occurs in the book of Proverbs. Proverbs is a textbook for a wisdom school. At one time there were wisdom schools, and the teachings were quite rigorous. We don't have wisdom schools these days. In fact the only wisdom training available now might be in a church or synagogue setting. I encourage you to read the book of Proverbs in the Bible and meditate on its wise instructions.

Having outgrown my years of praying for things, I now pray for wisdom. Consider the story of Solomon. As a very young boy he was to become king. God promised him anything he wanted. Of all the things he could have requested, Solomon asked for wisdom and an understanding heart. And God's reply was that since he had asked for wisdom, all things would be added unto him. In asking for wisdom, the great archetypal pattern, he was given access to all things.

The power of wisdom is also called judgment and righteous discernment. This is not the judgment of the ego, but the power of discerning right choice. We begin as children learning to tell right from wrong. Hopefully we learn simple things: don't lie but tell the truth, don't steal but learn to give instead, and don't hurt others but have compassion for they are part of you.

Being skilled at pulling this thread of wisdom through your to your adulthood requires focus and constant right choosing. Without it we fall into the traps of temporary gratification, attracted by whatever glitters. From learning this skill and focus, you will begin to discern what is Godlike and what is not, and to learn what will enhance your dream and your interaction with God and what will not.

Wisdom is the golden thread that you draw through your tapestry of life for success in all that you do. Wisdom gives you the ability to see to the heart of all matters, and to know what to do. Wisdom reveals what is really happening and speaks through you because you have asked it to. It brings peace and harmony into your world. It brings a true sense of oneness with the Creator all day long and forever.

Imagine if you will that you could go to your place of business, enter any meeting, and see to the heart of whatever was going on. Suppose you could look at a business venture and immediately know its possibilities and its faults. Spirit knows these things and spirit dwells within you. It is impossible to intellectually discern a wise decision from weighing physical facts. We have been taught to make a list of the pros and cons, and make a choice based upon that information. Even then, we still don't really know which is the wisest choice.

Here are some quotations about decisions based upon the best possible information of the time:

> "Heavier-than-air flying machines are impossible."
> —Lord Kelvin, president, Royal Society, 1895.

> "This 'telephone' has too many shortcomings to be seriously considered as a means of communication. The device is inherently of no value to us."
> —Western Union internal memo, 1876.

> "I have traveled the length and breadth of this country and talked with the best people, and I can assure you that data processing is a fad that won't last out the year."
> —The editor in charge of business books for Prentice Hall, 1957

> "Everything that can be invented has been invented."
> —Charles H. Duell, Commissioner, U.S. Office of Patents, 1899.

The best information of their time still did not help these people come to the wisest decision. We know now that the airplane, the radio, and data processing are foundational to our western world. Certainly, we have not reached the end of our creative inventiveness. In fact we are barely at the beginning because the divine wisdom of God within us is limitless.

So wisdom is the key, my friend. Be wise and consider it well. Draw it into all you do.

CHAPTER EIGHT

LOVE

Why wasn't love the first thread selected? Surely "the greatest of these is love," as Jesus said. Love is the greatest, but also not the easiest to understand and handle in our lives. How many broken love affairs do you know of? The rate of divorce has equaled if not surpassed the number of marriages in this country. How well are we doing just diving into love alone and hoping not to sink? We are not doing well at all. Remember that the threads must work together to support each other.

Love needs wisdom, right choices, strength, and faith. Oh, how we wish we had known this before we jumped into some of the situations and relationships that failed so miserably. Love is the thread we have a really hard time hanging onto. Time and again it slips away, or is wrenched away by fear, jealousy, petty problems, and misunderstanding. Our attempts at love often seem to create more separation than togetherness.

Our society is filled with twelve-step programs (there's that number twelve again) to help us reconnect with love of ourselves and others. We are taught to make amends where possible at the psychological and material levels. Ultimately we must, however, turn in prayer to forgive ourselves and let go of the pain. As mentioned in utilizing our life story, we can neutralize the emotional impact of the past by understanding that we all do the best we know at the time, and prayer helps us find the thread of love again. Since that capacity for love comes from God in the first place, then it is logical to go back to God to find it again.

After being involved in Unity "new thought" for several years I became aware that the thrill and excitement about it had waned. I was still very much interested in Unity teachings and taught classes, but as I watched new folks discover it and become enflamed with it, I began to wonder where my fire had gone.

I was researching materials for a class on the Book of Revelation and the letter to Laodicea jumped out at me. (Rev. 3:14) "You have left your first love. Return and salvage what remains or you will not be awake when I come!" That is exactly what I had done. I had left my love somewhere back there, my first blush, glow, and excitement at finding the truth that had set me free in so many ways.

I created a guided meditation for myself mentally returning to my first moments when that feeling had come alive. I visualized walking into the church, those with whom I spoke; and I stayed with the image until I could feel the excitement returning. I asked the feelings to all come back to me. Then I turned my visualization to the present and invited those feelings to come with me and live in my present world.

It worked! I had gathered up what remained while I could still remember it, and it awakened in me again. Whenever you have lost a thread, go back to where you remember having it last and pick it up again, just as you would a lost wallet. I believe this can be done in any situation you might have where the thrill of living has ebbed away. Married couples often return to a romantic spot from their past to rekindle their relationship. It doesn't mean that we live in the past, but that we reach into the storehouse of experience for what we need today.

Love is the cosmic glue that holds everything together. Without love our lives are fragmented. We can feel alone and disconnected. I remember being romantically in love. I felt expanded, empowered, supported, connected, joyful, and secure. The romantic love, not able to exist for long without the support of faith, strength, and wisdom eventually ebbed away and with it those expanded sensations. That sense of expanded life can return, if we will put the essential threads into place that make it all work.

In some societies the parents choose mates for their children. The parents have matured in faith, strength, and wisdom and are thought to be in a much better position to make a wiser choice than children who do not have the life experience. In our society children barely entering into adulthood are expected to make wise choices of a career, investments for the future, and a mate for life. Because we are on the cutting edge of freedom of choice in today's world, wisdom training would find a most needed place in our society.

Wherever you find yourself in relation to love today, be sure you have spiritualized your capacity to have faith, strength, and wisdom to support you as your love grows, fills you, and radiates out to your world. You spiritualize it by lifting up your thoughts and feelings about it in prayer.

CHAPTER NINE

POWER

"The mind and the body of man have the power of transforming energy from one plane of consciousness to another." Charles Fillmore

Philip is the disciple who represents the power of power. The name Philip means lover of horses. Charles Fillmore writes: "He represents the faculty in us that, through love, masters the vital forces ..." Philip was the evangelist and his word was charged with power. Mr. Fillmore locates the physical power center in the throat and it is that which "controls all of the vibratory energies of the organism."

Power comes quickly on the heels of the thread of love and power is the most feared, misunderstood, and misused of our gifts from God. Many have disavowed power entirely so as not to be categorized with those who seek it for wrong and destructive reasons. When we disavow a gift of God, we are in essence trying to negate a gift of God; but it cannot be done. It is an essential part of our being. Turning away from our responsibility to develop this gift properly is as destructive as allowing the ego nature to use it wrongly.

We hear a lot today about giving away your power and letting others have power over you. These are the result of not understanding the difference between spiritual and egotistical power. If you are in spirit in regard to your power, it cannot be taken away. You can abandon it, but it cannot be stolen or taken over. When you are in the ego mind set, where needs and dependencies run your life, whatever power you believe you have is definitely up for grabs. It is an ego game, a psychological dance, in which one endeavors to gain the most influence. The one with the least psychological influence loses. This is not a fun place to be.

Women, minority groups including racial groups, have been claiming their power, demanding their rights, and equal opportunity with the majority in political power. This is a good and necessary step for a "kinder and gentler world." But the process must go beyond the outer symbols of power such as access to jobs and wealth. It must reflect a deeper spiritual reality within each person.

Power—true power—has to do with spiritual mastery in our practice of spiritual principles, and dominion over the kingdom of our own being. Spiritual power must be held with the utmost humility, supported by faith, strength, wisdom and love. In the book of Second Samuel, King David exults, "God is my strength and power; and he maketh my way perfect."

Our prayer, then, is to claim our spiritual mastery in regard to power. This is an important transforming thread without which the tapestry falls apart. Remember the twelve all need each other, so it is no wonder that life falls apart when we slip from true power into the ego power dance that the world loves and fears.

The thread of power cannot be taken from you, so treasure it and learn about it! Consider the scene between Pilate and Jesus, when Pilate said, "Do you not understand that I have the power of life and death over you?" I credit Jesus' forbearance by not falling down the steps laughing. He had just raised Lazarus from the dead, and Pilate thought *he* had the power because he could order an execution.

Spiritualized power is a great gift for good in the world and within our own being. Just as a car must have power to be a transportation vehicle, so we must have power to be a vehicle for God, or we are useless. God didn't create us to be useless.

Mr. Fillmore said that we must "amp up on the energy of God" until we are filled up and then "overthrow it into the power center" to produce spirit-filled words. This is the intended application of the gift of power. Our words must carry with them the vibration of spirit that will transform us, and go forth from us to change our world and manifest our good.

CHAPTER TEN

IMAGINATION

How many books must there be on the subject of imagination! Imagination is surely the most colorful and creative of these threads. It is the picture show, the art gallery, the media aspect of our being. Is it any wonder that folks want to start right in with imagining their good without preparing the way first?

Imagination is represented by Bartholomew, who was the sixth disciple called. He was behind a tree when Jesus called him, so it is said Jesus had to imagine seeing him. Imagination needs the support of the first five threads before it can be utilized in a productive manner.

Imagination is so powerful with so many facets, that it can run away with you. It beckons you to the farthest reaches and beyond, and then leaves you to drift in the open sea of possibility. Imagination must have the anchor threads that come before it to keep it on course and make sure it reaches a destination, which is to manifest your dream in your life experience.

Have you heard that some people have no imagination? It may appear that way, but the same gift is placed within every one of us. We are all created equal. We may not be born equal, and we may not use the gifts equally, but the gifts are equally there, awaiting our use of them.

Spiritualized imagination comes into play powerfully in visualizing and creating our future and our new way of being in the world. We cannot spiritually interpret our lives without it, for we must be able to see intuitively an expanded way of being.

Imagination misused by the ego nature conjures up images of terror and destruction. It brings up images of fear and failure. They are daymares instead of nightmares! We live our lives in fear, if we have used the imagination to create fearful images in mind. So just as we must choose our thoughts carefully, we must also choose the images they create just as carefully. A picture is worth a thousand words, and that is true. A picture makes a much deeper impression in our minds and is more difficult to erase.

If we pray and meditate upon the good we want, images will come from God Mind instead of fearful human ego mind. God's images are perfect, and will be completely appropriate to bring forth what we praying for. In Unity we call them Divine Ideas. They are divine because they are born out of the perfect archetypal patterns in the mind of God. They are perfect because God has only perfect ideas and patterns for our expression.

Charles Fillmore writes, "The Spirit of truth projects into the chamber of imagery pictures that, rightly understood, will be a sure guide for all people who believe in the omnipresence of mind. Everybody dreams, the great majority do not attempt to interpret …"

The fine line between insanity and genius has to do with whether we can keep hold of this powerful multi-dimensional thread in our tapestry. It takes a never-ending vigil to keep imagination aligned with the Divine and not let it run away. King David let his imagination get away when he saw Bathsheba bathing on the roof of her home. His imagination led him to order her husband killed on the front lines of battle so he could have her for himself. What was the price for this misuse of power? They were denied life, symbolized by their first child being stillborn.

Before employing imagination, check to see if you have faith, strength, wisdom, love, and power under the influence of spirit. If you are not sure, ask in prayer that this be done in you, and then proceed.

Imagination has within it the power of "life more abundant," as Jesus said. It's misuse has dire consequences. It's right use, it's spiritualized use, has glorious rewards.

CHAPTER ELEVEN

UNDERSTANDING

The disciple, Thomas, represents the power of understanding. He was called doubting Thomas because he was a reasoning person and required physical proof that the man standing before him was Jesus. Jesus did not hesitate to provide this proof by showing the nail holes in his hands. We are expected to use our God-given intelligence in all things. God intended that we should inquire, research, and satisfy our questions. The biblical promise is that nothing shall be hidden from us.

It is not too surprising that understanding should be right there to support imagination. This would have to be a sister thread in our lives to correctly interpret what we are seeing. Correct interpretation means that we avoid the pitfalls of misunderstanding. It is interesting to note that it is not love that brings compassion, but understanding. Someone who has been through the same misfortune you have will be more likely to have compassion for you, because they truly understand. Your loved ones, who may not have that experience, may wonder why you don't just snap out of it.

Spiritualized understanding drives out war, poverty, and all the ills of human society. The prayer of St. Francis of Assisi challenges us to seek to understand, rather than be understood. This is the thread that causes the pattern of our tapestry to reach out to touch and comfort.

To understand why evildoers do what they do does not mean they shouldn't be restrained from injuring others. It means that we find ways to help them understand that the presence of God is within them, and all they really desire is within their grasp. They do not have to injure others to get what they need. If this does not change them, then they must remain restrained.

Charles Fillmore wrote, "The history of the Israelites is a sort of moving picture of man's soul and body development. When we understand the psychology of the different scenes, we know what we have passed through or will pass through in our journey from sense to spirit."

The writings of the Bible are given to us that we might understand the process of human life. The Old Testament is about our psychological development and the New Testament is about our spiritual development. The physical temple of the Old Testament can be destroyed, but the temple of the Holy Spirit cannot.

In the physical/psychological nature we wander in the wilderness until we understand ourselves. The Israelites are said to have wandered forty years. Forty is a symbolic number that means "the time it takes to get the job done." We will wander as long as we have not completed the job of understanding. The prophets admonished the Israelites to change their ways from idolatry to God, from the worship of the physical to the worship of spirit.

Understanding our own motivations and our own feelings gives us command of our lives. As we move into spiritual thinking, the Gospels help us learn to track our spiritual progress. The question is, "How do we think as a Christ-like being?" To correctly understand the signs we are given, as we ask for guidance, is to rule the kingdom of our own being. Jesus said, "Follow me." It is up to each of us to understand his invitation. It is an invitation to follow him in Spirit.

Spiritualized understanding is discerning the Divine within us and applying it to every day circumstances. Pray for this understanding at the beginning of every day. "Ask and it shall be given to you."

CHAPTER TWELVE

WILL

The disciple, Matthew, was a wealthy tax collector, hated by all. Since tax collectors were paid only after they paid the state, Matthew added extra fees to the taxes the people owed. When he met Jesus, he wholeheartedly surrendered his mercenary activities, leaving everything to follow the spiritual path. The will, like taxes, is often used to impose something upon other people.

What a troublesome thread this is for most folks who misunderstand it and fear the "will of God." So, to help us out, this thread comes right after understanding. Will is our forward motion. Will drives our plans like a chauffeur. Spiritualized will becomes the will of God, because it brings forth the highest desire of our hearts.

It is also the power within us that we mistakenly use to force outcomes. We use it as will power, to force ourselves to stop some habit, or as willfulness to control another person whom we want to do our bidding. Most often will is the cause of our defeat until we put "ing" on the end of it. Yes, willing and willingness are the tickets to positive movement, change, and guidance. Jesus asked, "Are you willing to be healed?" Being willing for your good is the sweetest state of mind, as well as a most powerful one.

Will is one of those threads that tends to knot up. It takes some patience to keep it free and to pull it carefully through the fabric of life.

Many stories are told about giving your will, your power of choice, into another's keeping. One of the most famous is the story of Goethe's Faust. Mephistopheles appears to Faust, promises to be his servant, and bring him every pleasure. When Faust asks what the price is, the reply is that it will be minimal. "I will be your servant in this life, and you will be my servant in the next life." Mephistopheles gets control of Faust's will by capturing his imagination with a vision of the beautiful Marguerite. Faust doesn't understand that he is giving up his soul. Just as Faust is about to partake of his pleasure, Mephistopheles kills Marguerite and snatches Faust away.

Our will is sought after by advertisers who want to take our power of choice from us. Somehow the product never produces the promised pleasure and we have been, indeed, taken. Our will always remains free when we spiritualize it. When we turn it over to God, God always returns to us the perfect manifestation of our own heart's desire.

The will of God is simply the highest desire of your heart for your highest good. God's will is not an imposition upon us, or a secret plan that we have to struggle to unravel. The plan is only as secret as our minds are closed. Fear closes our minds and we have been taught to fear "God's plan." Trust opens our minds. Trust in God that nothing in the great plan of life is intended to harm you, deprive you, or make you unhappy. Jesus mentioned that it was not God's will that any of the little ones should be harmed. Remember you are one of those little ones.

CHAPTER THIRTEEN

ORDER

Not much is known about the disciple James of Alphaeus, who represents order. James is the English form of Jacob which means supplanter, the higher order that must supplant the lower order. There is indication that he might be connected to Thaddeus and Matthew, but we don't know for sure. Charles Fillmore places the power of order symbolically at the solar plexus, the universal place where all systems in the body are connected. The solar plexus is also the navel through which the child in the womb is simultaneously fed and wastes carried off in an orderly fashion, that the infant can grow to be born.

This is not the dull thread we might think it is. It is probably a background color, coarse and strong. The power of order doesn't mean put things in a row on the shelf, or clean up your room. It is Divine Order, which has to do with bringing orderly manifestation out of the primordial chaotic stuff. This is your power to bring forth a lifetime that is livable and orderly according to divine patterns. It is your power to bring forth the Divine Design of your life as you see it.

Order, according to the dictionary, is "approximate magnitude." It comes from the Latin "ordiri" which means "to begin to weave." The tapestry of life we are weaving has a design which follows orders of magnitude, the lesser to the greater. We begin life with the umbilical cord sustaining our infant body in a physically orderly way. We learn to put the alphabet in order so that we can mentally recognize written language. The centurian who came to Jesus to have his servant healed, spoke about giving orders to his soldiers just as Jesus gave orders to the healing powers. These are progressive magnitudes of the levels of order. The centurian knew about ordering armies and through that he could recognize Jesus' ability to order the cosmic forces. Jesus expressed amazement at this man's understanding.

The root word of order, "ar," has to do with artisan, the part of us that weaves the order of God into our being. At the very root of the concept of order is the artist bringing forth the pattern of life. In ancient times, language was the province of the priesthood. The words formed had a spiritual base. We take an ordinary sounding word like order and discover that it is rooted in spirit and has a greater magnitude of meaning that we originally thought.

We are charged with bringing forth a new order of humanity, of which Jesus was the prototype. He demonstrated the Christ level of being, the highest magnitude known to humanity. As he transformed into the next stage he was first seen by Mary Magdalene outside his tomb. She did not visually recognize him. In the book of Revelation is a description of the future being. It has "a countenance as glorious as the sun and a voice like many waters ... When John saw the resurrected Jesus, he fell at his feet as dead." The shock was almost more than he could bear.

You-in-the-future will be very different from you-in-the-past, just as you are very different now from your ancient ancestors who lived in caves. You have within you the unlimited potential to grow into a greater magnitude of being than you now experience. Scientists have said that we use only ten percent of our brain. How awesome it will be when we use the other ninety percent.

We are here to co-create with God worlds without end and wonders that never cease. We are bringing forth a new order of humanity that is spiritually evolved and living in more expanded ways. The chaos out of which we bring newness is the unformed stuff, substance, or as in Genesis, the "waters of the deep" of God. Just as God did, we move in mind upon the waters of the deep and bring forth living ideas according to our vision.

So much for boring order. It probably wouldn't hurt to clean up your room, however, just for practice. Smile.

CHAPTER FOURTEEN

ZEAL

Jesus had called nine disciples into service and was about to call the tenth, Simon the zealot. Simon represents our power of zeal and enthusiasm. Simon was from the low country in Canaan representing body consciousness. Zeal is a raw power that begins at the lower physical levels and is like a high-speed train that is always in danger of jumping the tracks.

I can hear the rockets of the mind firing up right now. Zeal and enthusiasm light up our lives, burning bright and hot. Without zeal everything goes flat and is not very interesting. The lack of zeal is a very depressing, and eventually deadly, condition. We need this power to constantly stir up the gifts of God, as the Apostle Paul put it. In Revelation 3:16, it reads, "I would that you were hot or cold. Luke warm I spew you out of my mouth."

Zeal can light up or burn up what we are doing. Zeal that is unchecked and without spiritual direction, can produce a scorched earth effect in our lives. It can send everyone around us running for cover.

Zealotry is a violent theology that believes in killing anyone who violates the fanatical ideals. There are many zealots in the world today. Holy wars are justified through zealot theology, or a zealousness for God beyond all reason leading to destruction. When zeal becomes enthusiasm, it is infused with God. It is "entheos," God infused in our zeal, not people creating zealotry for God.

Charles Fillmore writes "spiritual zeal electrifies the nerve substance, which breaks forth into energy. Thoughts serve as distributors of the vital substance ... Every thought and emanation of mind liberates some of this stored substance ... Zeal gives a mighty impulse to all things."

Zeal is a power that cannot be used alone. If you loose it raw upon your life it will destroy love, blot out wisdom and understanding, distort imagination, and literally destroy your life. It will make of you a genius or a disaster, depending upon whether you turn it inward to your relationship with God or outward unchecked. King David, in Psalm 69, cries out to God to save him from his own unbridled zeal.

Zeal is to be used like a highlighter, in delicate touches for enhancing and bringing something to the forefront. Many zealots in the world today think they are doing God's work, but they are doing ego's work. They assume that their fire run amok is God, but it could never be God. The largest part of zeal is turned inward as a passion to hear the word of God speaking to us. It is a fire that burns upon the inner altar of worship of the Most High. Zeal for God promises a life of light and well-directed energy that never runs out.

Zeal is the life impulse of God. Without it everything stagnates in a state of depression. What are these without enthusiasm: Faith? Strength? Wisdom? Love? Power? Imagination? Understanding? All lie fallow awaiting the spark of zeal.

Every one of us has the power to become a genius when we call forth our zeal through our spiritual nature in our chosen field of action. Extraordinary zeal in the accomplishment of some ideal develops what is called genius. Zeal and enthusiasm are just the impulse we need to carry our dreams through to fruition.

Zeal is the fire of God. Zeal is the fiery impulse of spirit infusing your world. The fiery impulse is within us to impel our lives in whatever direction we choose. So, light up your tapestry of life with this one, but be careful not to destroy it by setting it on fire.

CHAPTER FIFTEEN

PURIFICATION

The dictionary definition of pure is full strength, unmixed, clean, and free. When we are pure, as God created us, we are not mixed with our own lower creations. By this I mean we are not mixed with weakening ideas of being something less than we truly are. Purification is the way of eliminating those things that are destructive that we have mistakenly created in our conscious and in our lives.

Thaddeus is the disciple who represents the power of purification. His name means large hearted and courageous. When we are large hearted and courageous, we have the largeness to let go of fear and the courage to turn to our God-given nature. The opposite of this is stinginess, which causes constriction, which stops the flow of life, and results in pollution.

When the waste in the cells of our body is not removed completely, the cells deteriorate and die. Since our cells are programmed to release waste, it is our thinking and our false beliefs about ourselves that interfere with this purifying process. Charles Fillmore wrote "This is a fearful, clutching, holding-on state of mind. When the body becomes outraged by the buildup of toxins, it struggles to free itself from its unhappy condition."

"Blessed are the pure in heart for they shall see God." Blessed are you when you constantly choose what you will let into your mind, and when you constantly throw out what is unworthy. We see God by seeing the divine within ourselves. We must be able to see through an unclouded mind.

This power of purity is also called renunciation. We have tremendous power to "just say no" to all that keeps us from living our Christ nature. We don't have to put up with weakness, illness, fear, and chaos. None of these things are natural to us. These are forms that humanity created out of a fearful mind, and we must purify ourselves of them and set ourselves free.

This thread is the power of purification, that of renouncing all that is not Godlike or creative. This is a quiet little thread that doesn't get too much notice until it is not working. It is the quality control system that eliminates what must be discarded.

Our spiritual nature cannot be polluted, but our ability to remain in conscious contact with it can be blocked by impure thoughts and ideas. So we have to keep flushing out the negative, the false, the harmful error thinking that clouds our perceptions. If we could not somehow discard these things, we would have no hope of surviving, much less progressing. We would become refuse receptacles instead of channels for God.

So, how do we activate this power? We do it with a series of denials. These are not the psychological denials of pretending something is not there. This is the act of denying fear or error any power over our lives.

So we definitely look at what errors are operating in our minds and lives. We recognize them as destructive, and deny them further attention. We turn our minds toward the opposite of them, toward good, which negates their power. Error thinking gains power when we keep our attention focused upon it, when we worry about it, fret about it, and expand on it with frightening imagery.

If we are fearful of lack and poverty, we now deny those thoughts any more power over our lives, and turn our thinking to prosperity and fulfillment. As we pray, we image abundance in our lives and open the door to God's Divine Ideas of abundance to fill our thinking and be manifest in our experience. The blockage created by thoughts of lack is flushed away and thoughts of prosperity restore our purity. Prosperity is a Divine Idea, an archetype. The universe is a vast expression of God's abundant creativity. Lack is an error thought in the mind of humanity.

So along with cleaning up your room, don't forget to take out the mental and emotional garbage. Keep your tapestry clean, sparkling clear, and beautiful.

CHAPTER SIXTEEN

LIFE

The power of life is represented by the disciple Judas. Judas is known as the betrayer, the one who betrayed Jesus for thirty pieces of silver. Judas carried the money, the currency of the material world. Judas had misunderstood what Jesus' mission was. He was sure that Jesus would lead an army and overthrow the Roman oppressor. When Jesus didn't gather an army, Judas decided to force the issue. He was sure that the confrontation in the garden would result in Jesus overcoming the Romans and starting his own kingdom. But the kingdom Jesus spoke of was spiritual, not physical.

All we knew of life when we were infants were just the bodily comforts. We knew when we were hungry, tired, wet, too cool, or too warm. We were concerned with receiving food and comfort. Our teen years brought the influence of hormones. We experienced moods, sexual urges, self-consciousness, and insecurity. In our twenties we faced competition, struggle, terror, romantic love, lust, and reproduction. We must outgrow all of these if we are to find our spiritual nature. Judas died as Jesus was rising from the tomb. The Judas idea of life misunderstands our true nature and must die as the spiritual reality is resurrected.

Charles Fillmore wrote "The quickening life of spirit anoints the whole body and resurrects it into newness of life and substance, thus begetting the new creature in Christ."

We might be tempted to wonder why this capacity for life didn't come first. But consider how much must go into creating a life that can evolve into its highest spiritual expression. Life must have all of its components spiritualized, functioning and in order, to be successful. Life is too precious to waste by leaving out all the prerequisites and crippling its power to function perfectly.

This all-important thread of life has to do with more than heartbeat, breathing, and brain function. It has to do with generating life everlasting. When Jesus said, "I came that you might have life and have it more abundantly," he was talking about two aspects of life simultaneously. Life as we know it now and life as we can create it.

You could be leading your life spiritually to its eternal unfoldment, or you could simply be following it to its physical disintegration. Jesus was the symbol of ongoing expanding life, and Judas was the symbol of physical life going to its necessary conclusion. Thus Judas is the disciple that Charles Fillmore chose to represent life, life that cannot go on forever unless it is spiritualized. It is not the physical body but the spiritual body that we raise up.

The woman at the well offered Jesus the water of physical life, and he offered her the water of spiritual life that she might never thirst again. She ran to the village to gather everyone to come and hear this teaching and drink of this spiritual water. And so it is that we spiritualize each of our twelve powers that we might create a living tapestry of our lives. The number twelve signifies spiritual completeness.

Life is the thread that you draw through the whole pattern to bring everything together. You are not just existing in this life, but you are co-creating with God a life beyond what we now know. One prepares by drawing everything together into a newer and larger cosmic story that will carry you into a greater place. A place already prepared for your new expanded story awaits your arrival.

CHAPTER SEVENTEEN

CREATING YOUR COSMIC STORY

"I go to prepare a place for you ..." Jesus Christ

Jesus was clearly indicating that there is more for us to experience, and a place must be prepared for an advanced experience. He didn't say what that was, but one might be tempted to think that he had done this before. There are indications that he was somehow father of us all. Perhaps he also prepared this place in which we now dwell.

Rev. Georgiana Tree West, Unity Minister in New York during Charles Fillmore's time, asked Mr. Fillmore who Jesus really was. Mr. Fillmore's reply indicated that Jesus was from "an advanced life wave" who returned to help humanity when it was in great peril. The light of consciousness was almost extinguished by ignorance, and he came to rekindle that light so we could go on. If there are more dimensions of living beyond the one we now experience, this may be what he meant by an advanced life wave. This could mean another life beyond physical death that is closer to godlikeness in its expression.

The disciples wanted to follow him and he told them they were not yet ready, but that they would know the way when they were ready. All of this indicates that we have something to learn, an inner knowledge of the way, and a place to use our advanced understanding. Jesus was the wayshower and we must "do the things he did and even greater things."

It is all a great mystery and yet it is a fabulous promise. This lifetime and this earthly experience are but a tiny segment in the continuum of eternity and we must use our most creative thoughts to have even an inkling of what that might be like.

We also must go far beyond familiar thoughts to prepare a place for ourselves to live. It must have more expanded possibilities than the one we previously created for ourselves, known as our past, for our future will be just as large as the story we create.

The Bible is a cosmic story, which contains the spiritual, physical, historical, psychological, educational, and legal aspects of human life. It is large enough to cover everything including where we were before we were born into bodies and where we go when we leave them. These are mystical places known as the Garden of Eden and the New Jerusalem. The Bible includes everything that could happen to humanity from the garden to the New Jerusalem, in graphic detail.

There is no need to rewrite the kind of detail already in the Bible. Your part is to write your own personal cosmic framework into which you will fit your own experiences, questions, dreams, mysteries, and goals. It needs to come out of your fantasy life, childhood dreams, and the highest aspirations of your heart. Keep it in the story telling mode. It might be helpful to begin with "Once upon a time ..."

The requirement is that your story be large enough to encompass anything that can happen in your lifetime, including being born and dying. You are able to create something larger than your life because you *are* actually larger than your life and experiences. You have within you the resources, though you may not yet realize it.

Why do this? The answer is you have a very important spiritual mission to accomplish: To awaken to your true nature so that you can partake in the eternal unfolding life God intended for you.

The way to awaken yourself is to begin praying for an idea. Pray for expanded sight and understanding. God gave you intelligence and the choice of your thoughts. These are your tools to awaken, so you must use them the best way you can. Spiritual guidance will come to you as a result.

To start "preparing your place" you begin writing a description of it. Starting with "Once upon a time ..." will help keep you out of the practical and mundane thoughts, and shift you into a fantasy world. Your story should describe a place you have never seen, but provides an explanation of why things happen and what they might mean in a larger, more universal sense.

You may not be able to write the story from beginning to end at first. You can start with a bare bones outline. Fill it in as your thinking develops about it. You will need to test it with life's difficult questions. As you read in the conversations of the class members in earlier chapters, you will expand the story until you have them all covered.

Does your story explain about the existence and purpose of war, illness, and misfortune? If not, then it needs to be expanded to include the reason these things come to be in one's life and, especially, what they are for. Try to explain everything within the framework of your story. If something doesn't fit, pray for wisdom, and make your story larger.

I know this sounds like work. But if you stay asleep in the physical unconscious, you run the risk of leaving the life wave that we are all in together. We fall behind and, like failing in school, we start over in the same grade with the group coming up behind us.

The Bible tells us to move quickly into this enlightened mode and be ready when the shift comes. I don't pretend to know exactly what that shift entails, but I do know that I love being in tune with God's life and joy. I want to get on that bus when it arrives and go to the next dimensional experience of life!

Self talk is essential in your spiritual growth. It is your most powerful life changer. Your mind chatters on with or with out your awareness of it. It is a problem solver, and if you don't give it something to good work on, it will find something out of your past to chew over. Talk to yourself about your spiritual nature until your mind learns to move into new habit grooves.

Most often we are self-critical. This critical talking goes on in the mind continually and does a great deal of damage to our self-esteem and our outlook. We make the choice to focus it Godward or to tear ourselves down. The world encourages us to tear ourselves down so it can take our power away and sell us products that are supposed to build us back up. You must resist that temptation by turning toward spiritual thinking, spiritual words, and spiritual plans to support your development.

Learn to describe the indescribable part of yourself. You need to create a spiritual vocabulary for yourself, such as the following:

Spirit—The invisible life of God within me.
Light—spiritual understanding
Energy—Level of God activity in me
Higher Vibration—God thoughts
Divine Guidance—Inner wisdom
Alignment—Congruency in our thoughts with God Mind
Intuition—Knowing that doesn't come from reason
Centered—Living from Spirit within
Empowerment—Spiritual power from God
God's Love—Universal, Unconditional
Co-Creation—Conscious co-creating with God
Regeneration—Reclaiming subconscious mind from destructive negative thought habits
Evolution—Unfolding in the likeness of God
Universal Being—Christ, our interface with God
Awakening—Aware of our spiritual nature

Christ Nature—God's perfect idea for every person
Substance—Spiritual basis of everything in form
Archetypes—Perfect patterns of God in creation
Spiritual Principle—That which is universally true regardless of time, culture, location.
Source—God the Creator, Sustainer, Unlimited, and Eternal.

This is not necessarily a complete list. You may find other terms you like that fit your experience. You may have different meanings for these terms. These definitions are ones I use, gleaned from years of studies. Just be sure your words and definitions are God based.

It is important for you to learn to talk to yourself about the invisible spiritual You, and to see yourself in terms that are beyond the mundane of the physical world. A common practice is to speak of ourselves in psychological terms. I no longer think about my I.Q., but about the Universal Mind that I am now learning to use. This takes me far beyond any intelligence quotient that a test could measure. We are unlimited beings in potential because we have this God-given access to God Mind at any time for anything. We find that we are geniuses as we move higher into spiritual ways. Why would God create anything less?

Do not be concerned whether your interpretations will be right or wrong. There is no right or wrong. There is simply your expression at the place in your understanding you have achieved so far. This is an individual spiritual journey, not a contest. You will not be graded or ranked. You will be lifted up to greater understanding than you now have.

You are right in the middle of your journey, and everyone else is also in the middle of theirs. Don't bother to compare yourself to others to see who is farther along. There is no such thing. You may be an old soul learning new things, or a new soul learning ancient things. Only your soul knows for sure, and it is not your spiritual business to worry about it.

Once you begin to develop a vocabulary, start using it. For instance, when you are feeling down, your vibrational rate slows down. When you are emotionally down, your mind is sluggish and your body feels heavy. This is not a godlike place to dwell.

You will want to return to a more godlike state of mind quickly. Begin by talking to yourself about your relationship to God and your spiritual nature, which is the truth of your being. Whatever has gotten you down will lose its power over you, and you will feel empowered once again. It is amazing how quickly your mind will turn you around. The key is what you are saying to yourself!

By interpreting our lives, we begin to discern the Divine Design for our lives and our expanded being. This is the point at which intuition and intellect connect. Intellect forms a verbal framework and intuition fills it with wisdom. At just the right time, spiritual knowing dissolves the framework and leaves us with a new freedom and expression. This expression is Christ in us as Pure Essence.

What will we know? The Bible says we will be "changed in the twinkling of an eye." We will know what is on the other side of that twinkling. We will know what we look like in the next dimension or evolutionary level of existence. We will know that we are still safe in the Creator's eternal plan. We will know the end of the power of earthly anxieties and fears.

To interpret our lives is to continue the creative plan for human life, the Divine Design. At this point we begin our conscious participation in the weaving of the design into a life tapestry.

"God gives thread for a web begun." God began the web in the "beginning" and we take the threads and pull them through, weaving them in and out as our experiences unfold.

At any given time in your life it may seem that something is missing in your experiences. It may be that the thread of faith is weak, or that love isn't clearly understood. You can refer back to the chapter on that thread and strengthen it as you need to.

CHAPTER EIGHTEEN

COSMIC STORIES FROM STUDENTS

The Cosmic Story is not as hard as you might think once you catch on. After you work with a few events from your life, you will start to do it in your head as you go along in life. Then your whole world will look different because it becomes the Cosmic Story in which you live deep in your heart. It is the avenue of your relationship to God in all areas of your life.

L. I'm not sure I believe in reincarnation. Who created God?

Author: Again start with "Once upon a time …" rather than huge hard questions like "Who created God?" Those hard questions will stop you in your tracks. And it doesn't matter if you believe in reincarnation. What matters is to get the story started and see if that idea fits as you go along. In other words, don't block yourself by trying to answer questions at the outset. Write the story.

V. I was a bit bored with my life story, but this was fun. A really exciting fantasy.

Author: Your life story is your past. Of course your future as an expanded cosmic experience will be much more exciting.

V's story: "A Child's Story"

In the beginning when there was only light, the universe was filled with intelligence and the Intelligence was with God and the Intelligence was God. And God became aware of herself and began to look about and began to experience different aspects of herself. And God spoke within the intelligence and asked the question, "Who among you would like to be in form and I stepped forward and was born into Spirit.
In spiritual existence, all was perfect for there was perfect love and perfect union and perfect peace. As we grow with God, God is our Father and Mother. We lived in her womb and in his belly, which is called Heaven. All was beauty.

There was no time and no death or decay. In Heaven every creature had a voice and everything could speak. The flowers, trees and animals would sing in unison "Glory, Glory, Glory great God Almighty!" And there was laughter that permeated the universe and music was far more beautiful and we danced with each other.

The joy of God was creation. On a great sea of glass ... and in Heaven there was no such thing as separation and the glory of God was intelligent.

And God spoke again and asked the question, "Who among you would like to be an explorer?" and I came forward and was born into a body.

Author: Great beginning! How does the concept of war fit into God exploring?

V. Opposition in all things. Opposites. Oneness gets split apart so we can look at it.

Author: What do you see as the condition of humanity today?

V. Perfect!

Author: Relative condition?

V. Humanity just doesn't know who they are.

Other students join in.

S. I'm trying to reconnect with God and trying to figure out what happened and how to get back. I feel like I'm struggling. I'm an intelligent being, but I'm having a lot of trouble figuring out how I got here. I'm a good person. Why did I get abused as a child? How did I suppress it? Why am I falling away? What is God going to do for me? I'm swimming in darkness seeking out the light.

D. I see the planet struggling toward the light. It is happening to people everywhere. And they're exhausted by the struggle. I crashed and it's a gift that I have this time. Swim upstream. Keep swimming. Every stroke I take, something new happens.

V. It's perfect, a good thing when we crack. I don't see a negative there.

Author: It is part of the human process. It is the only way we get outside of our structure of knowing. It all comes apart and for a while we are trying to gather up the pieces of it. But those pieces may not be appropriate anymore. It's an interesting commentary on humanity, that we hang on so tightly, build up so much and crash, so that we can be free to swim upstream. Weave this in as part of your cosmic story.

Think over what your beliefs are about humanity. At the absolute level it is all perfection; but if you said that to someone who just lost her child in a gangland shooting, where would the perfection be? It is perfect that you know the truth about that, but also explain the darkness. What kind of situation has humanity gotten itself into?

C. I struggle with an idea and it dawned on me that I had the notion within me that mankind is limited. We can only go so high, that we don't have the ability to go higher in the intellect. There is the All; and the more we try to get there, the farther away we get. We make it when we stop trying. We have to expand but we don't know where "up" is.

I believe we can move up with all our experiences. I did that. I made it, I survived it and I'm over here now until something else comes along. There is a path, my theme. It is all an accelerated process to God.

Author: How does it fit with people who don't seem to progress?

C. They're not ready to move up. They have the chances, and opportunities come along for them. They are working through something different. Some work through poverty. They get opportunities, but they may not recognize them. They can make the best or the worst of it.

D. When you read the Bible, you can see how far we've evolved in understanding meaning. That's a big issue now. We started from scratch, living in caves. And we've evolved to thinking about meaning. What is our relationship to God? What are our values? What is our purpose? What am I really here for? What does all this mean to me? How will this affect my evolution? This is big for me right now.

Some are still struggling in caves of confusion and doubt. We have all been through that struggle at different times. I just want to know the meaning of my situation. How do I get past this and move on to the next level?
We can see how the students were beginning to ask the larger questions and experience the desire to know more. There is always some frustration when we try to move forward in our thinking. The Apostle Paul said "I strain toward the upward call ..." We must reach beyond what we already know. We are spiritually evolving from the events of the past into explaining the present situation in a way

that frees us to create our future. The reward is the excitement and thrill of being a co-creator of the future. A new future that is not just a disappointing rubber stamp of the past. If we leave our minds to remember and mull over the past, that is what our future becomes. If we move our thinking on into something brand new and exciting, that is what our future will become.

APPLICATION

Your cosmic story. Go back to the first two pages of this chapter to refresh your mind on what it is that we are attempting to do.

(1) Now begin to write your own cosmic story. Remember to start with "Once upon a time ..." or at least use that state of mind so you can be free and unrestricted by "reality" and the usual limitations you've imposed on yourself up until now.

Remember, if it starts small or seed-like, it will get larger and will be stretched this way and that as questions come to mind about life and its events. You can start with my story if that would help. Use it as a pattern and modify it to suit yourself as you go along. Once again, don't expect to do this in twenty minutes.

This process starts with putting down on paper your rationale for why things are the way they are. We used to call it your philosophy of life. Since you are going into a cosmic or more expanded view, this will have more spiritual reality than a mere earthbound philosophy. I'm suggesting that you write as much as you can now because it will play a larger role later on in this book. Try not to censor yourself with "that's too silly" or "that isn't right." Try not to imagine others looking it over with approval or disapproval. This is very personal and no one else need ever see it.

(2) After you have completed step one, pick one event from your life history, one that is not too complicated.

(3) Take a quiet moment to close your eyes and ask to have the essence of this event revealed to you. Let the event speak to you as if you were an observer. Try asking it questions such as "what were you trying to tell me?"

(4) Go back to your cosmic story and see if there is a place that it fits in. Is there a higher reasoning for what happened? If it doesn't fit anywhere, why not? This will tell you where your cosmic story is too limited and needs to be expanded. Perhaps someone in your event died very young. Where in your cosmic story will you explain why someone might die young? Or perhaps you were trying to achieve a goal and were unsuccessful. How do you explain the meaning of these in your cosmic story?

This is what is meant by stretching and expanding your story to cover all eventualities. It doesn't matter if your explanation is right or wrong according to some worldly standard. Your explanation may even change as you grow in understanding. Keep the cosmic story fluid but cohesive. Eventually it will cover anything and everything that can happen to a human being.

(5) For assistance, look over the vocabulary list in regard to this event. It can help you see the invisible presence of God moving in it. If it has to do with money, you can look over Source, Substance. If God the Source is behind everything in form, then money must have a spiritual aspect and respond to thought. What were your thoughts in regard to money when this event happened? Some people have been taught to hate money, which chases it away. Some fear money, which shrivels and lessens its prospering effect.

(6) Were there destructive thinking habits influencing things? If you can see your mental part in the event, you can have command over future similar situations in your life.

(7) The goal for you is Godlike understanding. So pretend that you are an observer floating far above the event. Detach yourself emotionally. It might help to pretend that you are Father and Mother God seeing your toddler, your beloved creation, trying to make life work. We are all toddlers in this respect.

(8) Discover how empowering it is to take this perspective. Notice how good it feels to be a loving cheering section for this little one, instead of a frightened critic.

(9) How many of the threads of life can you find running through your event? Which ones are they and what part do they play? Which ones needed to be there and weren't? Strength? Were you not strong in your handling of finances. Was it understanding that was lacking? Was there a lack of faith that something good and prospering could happen to you?

(10) Repeat number two with as many events as you wish and take them through the process. The more you can practice with the events already encountered, the more you will be prepared for future events.

As I mentioned earlier, take some time with this. Read the paragraphs and sections over several times to give yourself a good foundation. Subsequent chapters will take you much deeper into your experiences, and it will all be more meaningful if you have some of this under your belt!

You can see from the student's sharing that we all struggle to know ourselves and to understand what is happening in the classrooms of planet Earth. Every event is a classroom in which we learn a life skill.

From here on we will build on what we have already started. Tools and insights will be presented for your consideration. Some will concern spiritual things and some will concern everyday things. As you read on, check back with your cosmic story and see how you might expand it some more. Eventually you will not need to put it on paper unless you want to. It will start to live and expand in you, and you will be glad for it.

CHAPTER NINETEEN

GETTING OUT OF THE SWAMP OF CONFUSION

Eve and Who?

Running through life's garden,
In laughing flowers and leaves,
I tripped upon a person
And fell down to my knees!

Whatever could have happened?
My feet I could not see?
When I stepped a bit too rapid,
Round about an apple tree.

Someone else was present,
I thought was just like me;
Sharing pathways never meant
Alike in expression to be.

So here I am bewildered
And faced with a decision!
I turn my focus inward
To find an answer, a vision.

Author

Life experiences are confusing. Things don't make much sense. People we thought were friends do unfriendly things. Industry ruins the environment to make money. Where will they spend it if there is no inhabitable planet in which to spend it? Warring factions pulverize their own civilizations in the name of God or saving their country.

Man's inhumanity to man is incomprehensible. Our confusion about all of this is a sign of intelligence. Confusion is not necessarily a sign of stupidity.

The Course in Miracles says that the world was created by an insane mind, the insanity of the ego, so don't even try to make sense of it. I happen to agree. Instead we want to make sense of our response to it and our ability to work sensibly to create our own productive experience.

Someone once told me that life is not fair. We just have to learn to be fair in it. Since I couldn't make life fair, this gave me a direction in which to move constructively. I could learn to be in command of my responses and be fair with myself.

Some readers may remember the self-awareness seminars of the seventies when we were just beginning to study self-esteem and its effect on our interactions with others. We practiced new responses to situations. We had family plays where the group would take the roles of the family members of the person practicing. The person would tell us how their family usually acted and we would do our best to duplicate the situations. The practicing person acted out their own usual way of responding to family members. Then we would encourage the practicing person to act out the way they really wanted to respond. They could clearly see how their new response changed the situation, and after a few practices, they could use it in real life situations. And it worked.

We discovered that we could choose a behavior that would bring forth a desirable outcome. We called it taking our power back, being the hero of our lives instead of the victim. It set us free of some of the world's craziness because we actually had some impact on our own situations.

As long as we try to make sense of the world, we remain a victim of its craziness. It keeps us dangling on a string. Like a grade "c" late night movie, we keep watching because we think it has to get better. It never does. It just commands our attention to try to make sense of it. It drains our energy, and gets us nowhere.

HELPFUL CLUES

I realized I needed to be in command of my reactions and my behavior, regardless of what the world was doing. Taking full responsibility for our actions is a good moral approach, and worthwhile, but the confusion about unfairness is still there. Unfairness is always in the back of our minds. Why me? Why this? Why do bad things happen to good people? Does the right ever triumph?

The answer to the last question is yes. Right always triumphs, but not at the physical/psychological level. At this level, it is a value call as to what is right, or who is more right than others. A right in one society is a wrong in another.

Right always wins when it takes the form of correct use of spiritual law in our thinking and living. Righteousness, right-use-ness of the law, always results in the highest and best for all concerned. Right always wins when we rise in our understanding to see the meaning of our place in events. This is right use of spiritual law.

After my third divorce, in chatting with another metaphysical student, we commented on how high the divorce rate was. He said that we are getting through our lessons much more quickly than in the past. It doesn't take us a lifetime or more to learn just one lesson now. The divorces aren't because of mistakes in choice of marriage partners. We choose the partner who has the lesson we need to learn, and then move on, if moving on is appropriate.

It was from that point on that I felt that I could in good conscience write thank you notes, not only to my former spouses, but former boyfriends as well! I could bless them for what I had learned about myself in the mirror of those relationships. I could get beyond the pain involved and bless myself for having the courage to choose and choose again.

TRYING TO GET OUT OR OUT TRYING TO GET IN?

We think we are of the world, and it is so painful that we try not to be in it. The solution we seek, however, is actually the reverse. We need to be in the world, but understand that we are not of it. How so?

When we think we are of the world, for example born as only physical beings out of others' bodies, our perspective is "from below" as Jesus put it. When you are trying to see from below, everything gets in the way and blocks your vision. Consider the toddler who sees only legs of tables, chairs and people from down there. It must look like a forest of obstacles! It is really hard to see the whole picture from there. The same is true of our belief about ourselves and what we are.

When you see from above, you are looking down from a high place and can see a very large area. I love to fly over the country in a jetliner, and see the miles and miles of mountains, fields, water and the continental shelf under the water at the shoreline. What a view of the world! And then we began getting pictures from space. Many of us at that point fell in love with our beautiful blue and white planet all over again in a much greater way. From that high place in space, there were no borders, no differences, and no confusion. It is just one unified and beautiful place.

BOTH SIDES NOW

We are multi-dimensional, multi-level beings. Part of us is visible, part invisible. Our power comes from the invisible part. We are taught to believe that power comes from money, position, friends, family, good looks, muscle, etc. But you can think of cases where people have all of these things and are still fragile, frightened, and confused.

When we understand the scope of our being, physical and nonphysical, we discover that we can work in the world, enjoy physical and material life, and still live in the greater dimension of spirit. God isn't confused, and when we are in our godlikeness, neither are we.

From on high in consciousness, Earth looks rather like a school where so many things go on all at once. Many different classes are taking place simultaneously. If everyone is at varying degrees of learning, we can understand why the world looks so disordered from below. If we take our clues solely from the chaotic physical/material level as to what our behavior should be, and measure our well-being from that, we lose track of the bigger picture.

One day it is a sin for Catholics to eat meat on Friday and the next day it is no longer a sin. Did God change His/Her mind? No, mankind did. For Protestants it was never a sin, so who is right? Who is wrong?

Right and wrong are man's perceptions, not God's. Choosing between what is Principle and not Principle is the ultimate reality. Seen from a higher perspective, each group of people is in a different classroom experience, involved in different interpretations of life. When we decide that only our own interpretation is right, we draw ourselves down out of the spiritual understanding to the lower psychological chaos and there is a conflict. Churches fight and split over these lower perceptions. Denominations point fingers of condemnation at others. Countries go to war at this level.

Was the Gulf War over oil, money, power, religion, freedom, human rights, borders, sovereignty, race, or cultural differences? All of the above are true at the physical/psychological, or lower vibrational levels. However, from above it was humanity scrambling around in the three-dimensional world clinging to lower level things for an identity that can only be found in God.

All of our strivings are an attempt to find God. All of our classrooms are an attempt to experience God in different ways. Some are vibrationally high, or spiritual. Some are vibrationally low, or physical. But it is all a search for God, and who we are in God. We stay at the lower levels to search only when we don't know it is God we are seeking,

POWER AND CONTROL

The most popular three-dimensional notion is that power and control equal survival, success, happiness, and the good life. Power and control at the physical level are subject to so many variables and unknowns that it is rather like riding an unpredictable bronco and trying to hang on to it. Sooner or later you will be thrown off.

All of life's energies are spent trying to stay on top for as long as possible. This is the stuff of our daytime soap operas. No one and no thing is trustworthy for very long at the lower levels. Love does not really exist here, and relationships are for convenience and profit of some sort.

Jesus showed us something else, the higher aspect of power and control. Change those two words to empowerment and command and you begin to understand at a higher vibrational level. Jesus had command of the empowerment that spiritual law offered him. The story of the temptations is a clear illustration. Jesus simply knew where the true power lay, and the proper use of it. He was not fooled by the appearance of power that was offered to him at the material level.

Often we are able to stay with spiritual empowerment while in meditation or in harmonious experiences, but when a terrifying appearance presents itself, we meet the test. If we have a financial set back, we quickly look to the outer world for a safety net, a way to recover. We can slip into blame, fear, entitlement, and anger, none of which will stop our fall or help us. Our true safety is to immediately raise our vibrational level to spirit, and the unlimited Source from whence our help always comes.

It takes guts. It takes practice. It takes a powerful sense of who you are as an offspring of the Most High. When Jesus was distracted, and felt his vibration lowering, he went apart to pray alone to raise it. He immediately took steps to return to the likeness of God. Be prepared to do whatever it takes to keep your vibration high the moment you have evidence that you have slipped into fear.

A GIFT TO BE SIMPLE

Spiritual principle is always simple. God is always simple. The Truth is always simple. Confusion can be all around us, and it has no power over our lives because in God we cannot be confused.

When we are confused, things have usually become complicated and we are turned around and around. The physical/psychological world is full of intrigue, half-truths, hidden agendas, fears, and power plays. This is the nature of the lower level. Don't blame the level. This is its lesson. When we lower our thinking with fearful or negative thoughts, we become subject to the contents of that lower level. We become embroiled in it when through our thinking we lower our vibration, and pull ourselves down into that classroom.

When we pray, the gift from God is simplicity and clarity. Prayer and meditation raise our vibrational level and keep us in a clear state of mind. Prayer thoughts and a meditative mind atmosphere are the way to the highest consciously attainable state.

King David, in the twenty-sixth Psalm writes of standing on a level place. We are to keep our heart and mind in the level place of God. We are vindicated by God when we do our best to stay in a high state of mind.

Verse 1— "Vindicate me O Lord, for I have walked in my integrity."

Verse 12— "My foot stands on level ground …"

When we walk in our integrity, fully integrated into Spirit, we do the very best we know how. We have integrated all the good we know into our lives.

If we could track it on an E.K.G., the vibration of God is so fine as to appear as a straight line. So when we are in our godlikeness, we stand on that level plane of God consciousness. We know where we are, who we are, and whose we are.

King David moved out of the lower vibrations this way:

Verse 4— "I do not sit with false men. Nor do I consort with dissemblers, … and I will not sit down with the wicked."

He kept his mind in higher realms of thinking:

Verse 6— "I wash my hands in innocence, and go about thy altar, O Lord, singing aloud a song of thanksgiving and telling all thy wondrous deeds."

This is a wonderful Psalm to study. It is simple and clear as to what we must do and not do. And it is clear what God does. It is God's job to vindicate you. It is not the job of your striving ego, personality, willpower, or cunning. Once you have returned to the higher realms, you are not available to the influence of lower vibrational contents, and this is your vindication. It is automatic. No begging, convincing, or pleading your case. God is law. God is love. God is Principle, constant and abiding within you. Your return to God in consciousness vindicates you. This exercise will assist you in digging up the roots of your guilt and self-limitation. It helps neutralize their effects on your life and replace them with affirmations that state the spiritual truth about you.

APPLICATION

1. Make an inventory:
   a. What childhood circumstances did you blame yourself for creating, thinking "If I were just a better kid this wouldn't have happened. Mom and Dad wouldn't fight."
   b. What have you been short sighted about? Have you seen yourself only in the light of past failures? Are you actually doing better than you ever thought?
   c. What are you lacking? You are probably suppressing those things you think you are lacking because you have everything within you in spirit, ready to come forth when you recognize it.

2. Others do stuff that you take on:
   d. What has been done to you that needs to be released?
   e. Who do you need to release from your mind? Don't let them occupy your mind rent free and cause you further damage by keeping them there.

3. Stuff Happens:
   f. What circumstances seemed to entrap you? What did you walk into unwittingly, innocently, and become entangled in?
   g. How did you respond? Guilt? Anger? Resentment? Shame? Give up and fall apart?
   h. What did you learn about survival? (After all, you are still here.)

4. Take your inventory and create an affirmation for each negative one until you have turned them all around.

If you thought you were faulty:

> "I am God's perfect creation. The perfect pattern is imprinted on every atom and cell of my being."

If you thought you were guilty:

> "I am innocent in the eyes of God, my Creator, and I release myself from this incident and this person. I declare that others are who they are at the moment. Their behavior is not my fault and I am not diminished by what

they did. I release myself and everyone involved, and we are all free to grow in Truth."

If someone hurtful still lives in your mind:

"I forgive, release and let go of all people, events and emotional memories. I am free and ready to get on with my healing, my wholeness, and my life."

To move on:

"I am free from all past circumstances and the results of those events now and future. I ask the Holy Spirit within me to do this work in and through me now and always. Amen."

5. Read through the Twenty-Sixth Psalm. The Psalm writer, King David, has been through all the same things we have and he was still the beloved of God.

CHAPTER TWENTY

GOD BYTES

"The opening of your mind, heart, and life to the guidance of Spirit is the beginning, not the end of wisdom. Inspiration may come like a flash of light, but the teaching of the Spirit of Truth is steady and abiding."

      Martha Smock: Halfway Up The Mountain

Does God really talk to me and communicate with me? Does God tell me what to do, literally? I really don't want God to tell me what to do, except when I get hopelessly lost, of course. Tell me, where is the plan written for me and who is writing it?

Today we can go to a chain bookstore and find a book on just about anything. Books tell you how to do things, where to find things you want, and how to get rid of them. The information super highway is dumping into our laps an overwhelming cargo. The choices are already so vast that you must stay glued to your computer screen so as not to fall out of the loop.

God gives us exactly the wisdom and information we need at the moment we need it. God bytes! Like the computer, we need only to learn to access it, and like the computer it takes practice.

God's wisdom is always knocking on the door of the mind. It leaks in through the cracks in various ways until we become curious enough to open the door. The cracks are evidenced by the occurrences of:

FLASHES

This is a list of opening events from the simplest to the most complicated. Perhaps you have had moments when what you needed came to you in a flash. It was as if the obvious just lit up in your mind and you said, "Why didn't I think of that before. It is so simple."

You see, all knowledge is already yours. That is why it seems so familiar and is just right for what you need. A flash is a moment in consciousness when the door of your mind blows open and there it is.

It is next to impossible to produce the flash at will, but it is possible to systematically pry and prop that door open a bit more.

HUNCHES

Hunches are another way of accessing God bytes of information. We believe that hunches come from our human cognitions, from something we have learned on an inside track of some sort. They are a combination of a feeling, knowing, and gut reaction. So anyone can have a hunch that "pans out." When it does, it gives us a secret feeling of confidence at the lower vibrational level of "I told you so!" It puts the ego one up, so to speak.

A hunch is God speaking through us at the level in which we are functioning at the time. You see, God just keeps the knowledge coming to us. We get what we need at the level we are able to receive it at the moment. Neat, huh?

But this is not a very efficient system. Like the flashes, it is hit and miss. We stumble into an open place in our consciousness, and information slips through.

DREAMS

When we finally put the intellect to sleep, subconscious mind picks up the incoming messages and transfers them through to us in pictures and impressions. Dreams are often regarded as night fantasies and not of much importance to our daily living. So negligible do we consider them that we inadvertently train ourselves not to remember them. Then when we realize they are an important part of our lives, we have to retrain ourselves to remember them.

That training can include programming the mind with an affirmation that we will remember our dreams. We place a journal beside the bed to quickly write down any fragments or scenarios we can capture before they fade away. Behold, we begin to remember our dreams. Again, it takes a little time.

The next step might be to program the dream by posing a question to subconscious mind so it can serve up the answer in the dream. Believe it or not, this works. As a child I took tap dancing lessons for a short time. There was a step sequence I was supposed to practice before the next lesson. I couldn't remember it and I went to sleep trying to remember. In a dream I danced the step sequence and then I was able to practice it the next morning.

Since subconscious mind is not logical and linear, we have the task of interpretation. The messages are not always as clear as that tap dance step. It is helpful to learn something about dream interpretation, symbols, and what to look for in a dream.

There are many books on dream symbols, but ultimately you will have to decide what the component parts of a dream mean to you according to how you normally value, think, and feel about them. For instance, what does an automobile represent to you? Power? Freedom? Danger? Individuality? Self-image? Should one show up in your dream, what are the setting and the scenario. What are the actions taking place? What are your feelings in the dream? As you sort these things out in a journal, ask deep within yourself for the message to be clear. Your answers to these questions may reveal a surprising pattern. Sometimes several dreams in a row hook together to reveal a longer, more complete message.

All of this takes a bit of practice, but it is a fun and worthwhile adventure. It is a step in learning to interpret your life as it unfolds. Remember that symbols may be universal but they are also personal, so someone else's interpretation may not be right for you.

Try this. Determine to give every dream a happy ending. Make it correspond with an effort to choose a happy ending for each episode of your life. You may find that you can gain a certain amount of conscious control over your dreams at night and direct them toward a happy outcome.

You can train your subconscious mind to run in a positive and happy mode much of the time. I call it being consciously in charge of the kingdom of your own being, aligning with the Christ pattern within you.

We were all created from the Christ pattern. The Christ is God's perfect idea of humanity, but we have chosen by our error thinking to manifest something other than that perfection. It is like a pattern for a suit of clothes. If we follow the pattern exactly, the result will be just like the pattern picture. If we choose to alter it here and there, the result will be very different from the picture.

Nightmares, occurring in adults, are an urgent message that something within us needs attention immediately. You may want to consult a professional if you have recurring nightmares. You may have unreasoning fears, phobias, or things that deeply disturb you that may be causing mental stress or physical illness. A nightmare might also be the result of eating very rich food before bedtime creating gastric disturbances.

This does not include children's nightmares that are usually outgrown by age twelve. Soothing children's fears, however, or checking to see if something is amiss in their lives, such as illness or abuse, is in order.

GUESSES

We can build our confidence in using God bytes, bits of information, by the practice of guessing. Vrle Minto, in his Alpha Truth Awareness seminars, made use of this by having his students begin guessing about all sorts of things: who is calling when the phone rings, what color is the fifth car coming around the corner. Guess about everything and see how many times you are correct. Chances you are you will be surprised at your accuracy rate. You may begin by being accurate at least 65% of the time. The more you practice the more you trust yourself to access your potential for knowing beyond just the knowledge from past experiences and learning.

You are naturally tuned in, clairvoyant, and sensitive, but you have learned not to trust that information. It has to come from a famous author to be trusted. Well, who is the most famous author of all life? God, the source of your flashes, hunches, dreams, and knowing. We are more likely to trust a popular magazine writer trying to make a living through sensationalism, than the all-knowing God of creation.

There is nothing strange or weird about knowing things that come to you and trusting them. There are people who have cancelled an airline reservation at the last minute, and avoided a plane crash. What happened? It wasn't their time to check out, or there was no trauma coming into expression in their consciousness, so their path was diverted around the problem intuitively. Many people do this all the time, quietly aware, but without talking about it.

Kids love guessing games. It exercises their innate wisdom. We as adults love to guess, too, but have had to put it away as a childish thing. After all, we adults have to have empirical proof to be sure. We have to be right. We have to subscribe to worldly wisdom so that we aren't to blame if something doesn't turn out right. We so fear being thought fools.

If I am a fool, I am a fool for God, my Creator/Sustainer. I am going through eternity with my God, not with the outer world. My salvation, if you will, is in my ability to accept and read God bytes in my journey though all my experiences.

Why does God send us bytes or little pieces of information? God doesn't. God sends us the whole tamale. We have such a short attention span, assisted and encouraged by ten-minute television segments and fifteen minutes of choppy commercials, and our busy schedules, that we can hardly stay tuned in long enough to get the whole picture all at one time.

Our pace is fast, giving us time only for brief encounters, fast food, convenience stores, and mini-everything. We are easily bored and dash off to something more exciting. Thank God for the reverse influence of meditation, hiking, bird watching, beachcombing, and videos without commercials.

THE OPEN CHANNEL

Jesus was in constant communication with God, constantly interfacing with his divinity. He maintained an open channel for God to live through him. If the channel needed renewal, he went apart from the others so he could commune for longer periods of time. People crowded and thronged him when he made an appearance in public. His life was also fast-paced. But his commitment was to his interface with God, out of which came the empowerment to do everything he accomplished.

Jesus could see the whole picture. He could see into the minds of men and women. He knew people's hearts and could see their future. He spoke to them clearly about what they must do to save themselves from the results of their error thinking. He taught "not as one of the scribes" who read only what had been written, but "as one with authority." He spoke of God as if he knew God intimately, which truly he did. And so also can we!

We can read the minds of others, but not as a voyeur. We read as one who knows the energy pathways of being, as one who is in tune with the flow of energies, and who can see a direction that another is traveling. We can guess their future if they continue that particular pathway of thinking. We already know when such a person is on a path of self-destruction, of fear, and hatred. We know the pain they bring to themselves and others around them.

This is a general knowing. We can see the path of the strong, quiet, and loving. The storm will rage around them and they will not be disturbed. Blessed are the peacemakers, for theirs is the Kingdom of God? The peacemaker is a powerful, all-seeing person who harms no one. The peacemaker is first and foremost at peace within.

If we understand this much about the "mind of man," we can hone that skill by observance, prayers for wisdom, and a quiet trusting heart. If you are dedicated to spiritually interpreting your own life and the unfoldment of your spiritual nature, it will be given to you to know. Nothing you ask will be hidden from you. This is the promise.

God bytes connect to become megabytes and then whole vistas. It begins with ourselves and exploring our individual being first. You must grow and expand to this magnitude. The novice cannot handle this level of knowing without preparation.

One time I was in Corpus Christi on the intercoastal sand bar where the Gulf of Mexico spills into the intercoastal waterway. It was evening and I had walked out on a long jetty that reached into that intersection of water. The water was black and turbulent. The further I walked, the more rubbery my knees became. I looked out on the water and realized that the disciple, Peter, stepped out of the boat onto the stormy sea that must have been black and threatening like this. I gained a new respect for the Peter, the fisherman disciple.

At the end of the jetty, the waters were vast and wild. I raised my arms and shouted, "Peace, be still" out to the sea. I was too small, though, and too undeveloped a channel for the energy of God I was asking to come through me. I sank onto my knees. I then knew the magnitude of the work that I still had do on my own soul growth. Now I had a measure of the distance I had yet to go.

It wasn't discouraging, but exhilarating! I could see the journey ahead, and I knew the next steps. I could see the future, not in terms of human detail, but in the greater Divine Design.

I can now imagine Beethoven hearing the whole symphony in his head before he even wrote the first note. Handel heard the complete Messiah. As we open ourselves more and more to our own divine design, we will see the whole pattern in all its glory.

Is it a long path? I don't know. What is long and short in spiritual terms? Ignorance and darkness are interminable. Light and enlightenment are instant and eternal. What are you doing for the rest of your life, anyway?

Flash
Hunch
Dreams
Guessing
Being the Channel

APPLICATION

This exercise will help you recover some of the intuition you may have forgotten. We have wonderful intuitive events that give us a window on the greater capabilities of our minds. It will also restore your trust in your own ability to access knowledge waiting on the outer fringes of your thinking. We have been given such a wonderful scope of intelligence if we can take our focus away from the material realm to let that part express. Journal with words and/or pictures your God bytes:

(1) Keep a small notebook close at hand to record flashes, hunches, dreams, and any intuitive events. Begin by priming the pump with hunches, flashes, or dreams from your past that you can recall. Check through your life story to refresh your memory.

(2) Keep this journal for a month or so until you automatically pay attention and respond to a hunch or dream the moment it happens to you. Keep the journal until you have established a habit of noticing and responding.

(3) Journals help us acknowledge our insights in whatever form we receive them, and not pass them off as whimsy or unimportant. You may also find that several bytes in a row constitute a larger message. A larger message may unfold over a period of time and you can know that only if you are keeping a record.

(4) Write down a question you would like answered and read it over before you sleep. Make it something real. God doesn't work in hypothetical situations.

(5) Expect an answer. Write down whatever comes to you, even if it seems to be nothing. Sometimes I have asked a question that doesn't have an answer yet in my life, and I would get a blank. Even no answer is an answer. Consider it carefully in regard to your question and where your life is right now.

CHAPTER TWENTY ONE

MAKING SENSE OF ME

Sing to my heart in its solitary place.
Sing to its power and sweet hidden grace.
Great Silver Glory revealing your face,
To shine in and fill all the hollows and space;
Sing my heart out of its solitary place.

                        Author

We always have to make sense of ourselves first. Each of us has a solitary place inside that needs to be filled. We look for that fulfillment in other people, places, and things. We look for it in careers, relationships, and religion.

I didn't always know that only God could fill the void. It didn't know I was seeking God when I looked everywhere for fulfillment. I didn't always know I was looking for the face of God in everyone I met. I didn't always know I was an expression of God looking for my reflection in the eyes of others. I learned these things through a half-century of searching.

LOOKING OUT THERE

Most often we try to make sense of life, people, and the world by coming up with a code or philosophy that will straighten it all out for us. From sense to nonsense to illusion and back we run, each one sounding good in theory, but not in practice. Each one fell short for me. Sense or logic uses facts like building blocks that pile up perfectly and yet will not bring us to the truth. Nonsense or fatalism says that we live and die for nothing, and are destined to remain empty all our lives. Illusion or romanticism helps us we pretend that we are fulfilled, when we are really empty. Remember the song, "The Great Pretender?" Some of the words are

"I seem to be what I'm not, you see. I'm wearing my heart like a crown, pretending that you're still around." The ego mind leads us into all sorts of dead ends, promising fulfillment it cannot deliver.

I went back to college after fifteen years in and out of marriages, raising children and working many different jobs. I felt the void inside and chose a college major that would perhaps fill that. First I settled on philosophy. I soon saw that each great philosopher's idea held the seeds of its own demise. Their system would break down when stretched to cover the growing and changing world.

I turned then to psychology. From Freud to Skinner to Perls, I was again chasing the illusive idea that they could answer all of the questions of existence. Only Carl Jung could come close to it because he dealt with human spirituality. He called it Individuation, similar to our understanding of the Christ nature.

I had a superficial understanding of the Christ nature or the divinity within us. I still hadn't fully understood me. My last major in college was in the Interpersonal Communication department. It picked up on the self-awareness movement early and a whole curriculum was created around understanding ourselves. It was brand new as a college major, and it was a joy and a thrill to find it.

Students flocked to the program. Classes were packed. Here was something that spoke to a crying need among people. It offered tools and classes in making sense of me, making sense of human relationships and human interaction. Of course, we were ridiculed. We were dubbed the "talk, talk, talk" department. Folks thought that all we did was sit around and talk. That was partly true. But we were learning so much about ourselves, and how things we did and said affected others, how those things created our life experiences. What is going on inside you that causes your particular expression in any given situation?

LOOKING INSIDE

Robert Browning, in his poem "Truth Is Within" wrote about this very thing:

> "… to know,
> rather consists in opening out a way
> whence the imprisoned spendour may escape,
> than in effecting entry for a light
> supposed to be without."

What is this hidden splendor and how will we find it? How will we open out the way that Browning talks about? Where will we begin?

Feelings are created by thoughts, and they point the way to the splendor. They can tell us whether we are going towards, or away from the splendor that we seek. In order to open out the way, we need to look into our feelings. Feelings of fearfulness, loneliness, frustration and helplessness can stand in the way. In order to "open out the way" we need to move through these feelings, converting their energy from negative to positive. So we must begin with where we are. We cannot start where we wish we were.

To reduce the scariness of sifting through our feelings, we rise to the spiritual interpretation of our life events. It becomes less scary when we understand that we are here on this planet to learn, and metaphysics is the safest, surest way. We begin to dig through the rubble that has buried our light by looking at the thought that produces the feeling. We can change the thought that changes the feeling. Making even the smallest opening will let the light shine brightly through!

Negative feelings are like shadows on the forest path. They look like a bear until the light reveals them to be just a stump. Notice also how bright even a pinhole of light is in a dark room. Soon the whole area is aglow and transformed, and the splendor is ever more apparent.

"NO" TO YOUR GOOD

We unwittingly say "no" to our good. We keep our own good away from us. The Apostle Paul said, "I do what I would not want to do, and I do not do what I would want!" What part of me says "no" to my good? What part of me keeps me from doing what I want to do to improve my life? It is the part that:

> Says no to exercise for my body
> Says yes to harmful food
> Is lethargic when I am at home
> Wants to be disorganized and messy
> Doesn't want to plan anything
> Gives in to pining and loneliness
> Says it is all hopeless anyway
> Wants to blame circumstances

These are known as self-defeating behaviors. Self-defeating behaviors come from self-defeating thoughts and attitudes.

What part?
The part that believes that I have do to this all alone.

The part that believes I should know everything.
The part that compares me to others and finds me lacking.
The part that is afraid to live on the edge.
The part that is shocked and paralyzed by difficulties.
The part that I created in opposition to my divine nature.

I did this? Yes. As a child I created a shell around myself, in order to survive the adult world of expectations. I created places within myself to hide. These places were created out of lies about me that I believed to be true. I told myself there was something wrong with me, I wasn't smart, and I didn't fit. These were things I decided must be true because of the messages I got about myself from others. I hid from everything and everyone, especially a God that was supposed to be watching me and counting up my sins. My shell was my safety and my loneliness, my darkness and desperation.

It is out of these places where we hide, that we try to interact with the events of our lives, pretending that everything is fine. We are "cool." We are anything but cool, however. I watched helplessly as a high school classmate slid farther and farther into that shell, until at last he committed suicide. Even the love of a wife and child couldn't lift the darkness and despair in him.

INSIDE

It seemed that my life was a hopeless zigzag of experiences born of desperation, loneliness, and feelings of inadequacy. I threw myself into whatever the next step seemed to be, only to have it eventually end in some unsatisfactory way. Marriages ended. Jobs went nowhere. The hollow inside grew. I hoped each new opportunity would be "it", would be the splendor, and end my long trek in search of some sense of fulfillment.

Somewhere inside me there was someone special who wanted to express the splendor. She was my divine self. I couldn't identify very well with her, so she gave me her name. I have known her name since I was twelve years old. At first I simply thrilled to the sound of the name, not knowing why. Through all of my stumbling through life, she would call to me to pick myself up and keep on trying. I described her in a poem:

The Eyes of Rebecca

I've written a poem to everyone else,
Ignoring the longing inside

To have just one poem written for me;
Love, secretly to me confide.

I look in the mirror, my true self to see,
She's deep and lovely I know,
But I haven't seen what she says about me,
I hide all the things I fear show.

The eyes of Rebecca are looking for me,
My sweet inner spirit to outpour;
For I am the healer, teacher and priest,
And woman, yes woman, and more!

I long for the touch of a lover,
A smile and gentle support;
I've reached for so many an offering hand,
To find the door closed like a fort.

Is this the mirror of what I have built?
A citadel circling my heart.
Can I pry the gate open a bit,
And let love again make a start?

The eyes of Rebecca are looking for me,
The Divine in me calling my soul;
To the lover that lives deep within me,
And loves me until I am whole.

The call was from inside and would not be satisfied by something outside. I thought if I could find something outside, it would somehow creep inside, clear away the darkness and fill me up. But that is impossible. The world of form is the end result of an energy already spent. It has no life to give. An idea comes to fruition, takes form, and dies. Everything in form is dying, a passing monument to an idea already expressed and past.

SAYING YES INSIDE

Again, the way to "yes" to our good is through spiritual interpretation. It describes our relationship to God. Our ladder up out of the dark abyss is not an endless analysis of our stuff, but an interpretation of it that is helpful on our life journey.

The way to "yes" is to eliminate the fear ... fear that what is inside us is unworthy, phony, or that there is really nothing there at all.

A student in a class that I taught at a university approached me after a class in interpersonal communication. These were his fears also. He asked, "What if I get in there, get to the bottom of things, and I don't like what I find?" We are so deeply afraid of ourselves. It seems as if we believe we are monsters, as if God would create monsters or unworthiness!

We symbolize this with images of the boogie man. Children fear to go to asleep alone in a dark room. So deep in our heritage is this fear that it seems to appear even before speech. Carl Jung believed that these images have been with humanity for so long that they have become genetically encoded and are now passed along from generation to generation biologically.

How did this fear start in us? Why? I'm sure that original sin didn't have anything to do with sex. I'm sure it had to do with the first fears, perhaps symbolized by the forbidden fruit in the garden of Eden. We partook of the knowledge of good and evil, or the knowledge of love and fear. Before then it was just good and love. In order to have experiences, there had to be opposites ... dark and light, yes and no, good and evil, if you will. They constituted choices and our freedom to choose one or the other at each turn in the road. The eating of the fruit was our first choice away from God. From there many, many choices unfolded before us, and physical life experience began.

Understanding the depth of human fear tells us why merely reciting a few affirmations will not dispel them. The fears are perhaps something we will always have with us, but they don't have to control our lives. A fear is a wonderful signpost to tell us where we need to look to heal ourselves and return to God. It tells us where to look for the next opportunity for the splendor to shine through.

Through therapy and education we can begin to trim the foliage of this choking vine that has grown into every area of our lives. We continue the work until we find the tap root and dislodge it from its control of our consciousness. Once we sever the taproot, it no longer nourishes the branches of fear that have crept through our thinking.

I discovered in an error in my thinking the taproot of a fear that was destroying my happiness. When I would fall in love, I interpreted the pain of my uncertainty as ecstasy. Love was supposed to hurt! The romance magazines and books said so. "Waiting by the phone ... will he call?" So close are agony and ecstasy that I misnamed the feeling. It was actually agony! Out of this error I created painful relationships within myself and with others.

The branches of this evil plant worked their way into my career choices, family interactions, meditation times, as well as relationships. Agony legitimately had an upper hand in my life until I began to call it by its right name: Fear. Changes for the better then came quickly, because the tap root of that mistake was severed and the branches died away.

There is not a monster deep inside, but a badly maligned angel. I told the student at the university that the only thing I would guarantee him was he would love what he found deep inside himself. At the center of each of us is the Christ pattern for "being" that is created from the essence of Divine Love. It is our home, our bliss, our splendor. It is what we long for as we search in our relationships and life experiences.

> Illusions end, the curtain falls
> On barriers climbed a million times.
> Squinting through the clouds of pain
> No longer plagues our every day.
>
> How came we to this openness?
> So sound asleep we seemed!
> What lucky turn of destiny
> Dissolved the opaque veil?
>
> We learn to tread above the path.
> The light is truer there,
> For when we rise in consciousness,
> We are the light we share.
>
> Author

INSIDE OUT

All of this brings us to the truth of where our life and living comes from ... the inside out. Everything comes into our experience from the center of our being, then moves to the circumference. We stop living only on the surface. We stop drawing our cues about who we are from the outer world. The clues begin to flow from within, from an eternal source that never fails. Wisdom comes from the pattern of divinity deep within us and pours outward for use in our everyday lives.

The apostle Paul said, "Let the mind be in you that was also in Christ Jesus." This mind was the divine source of Jesus' wisdom and spiritual power. He was always interfaced with God, and not with the world. He drew from within to give to the world. We call his gifts miracles and his teachings miraculous!

We have the same opportunity as Jesus, to use the Divine Mind wherein dwells all wisdom and knowledge. We have the same opportunity to be constantly interfaced with the Creative Principle we call God. We have the same empowered spirit to do the things Jesus did, and even greater, as he promised.

But aren't miracles supernatural? Yes, they are, and so are we! We are spiritual beings inhabiting physical bodies in order to co-create with God a progression of experiences called a lifetime. We bring our lifetime out from within us according to what we generally believe about life. Everything comes from the inside to the outer. Miracles will not come from outside of us. They do not come from the world of hollow form. They come from the Divine Life within.

>I am grateful that somehow I know.
>I am grateful that there is more to know.
>I am grateful that in knowing God more,
>There is nothing else but God to know.

REACHING IN

In famous paintings of saints and holy ones, the eyes are often rolled up and back, as if the person were swooning. The artist is depicting them looking into their own souls, looking toward the presence of God within for guidance and inspiration.

This is where we begin to understand that meditation isn't just a fad, and contemplation only for the monks. They are essentials for every one of us on the spiritual search. We cannot step into the spiritual work if we are focused only on the outside.

Truth and reality are found within. Inspiration, wisdom, and answers to life's challenges and mysteries are revealed only to those who turn to the inner realm. We access this inner realm through meditation and contemplation. The following meditation will take you through a series of statements that support you in affirming your higher nature, your spirit. Affirmations are not wishes, but statements of spiritual truth about you. They always lift you up out of the mundane, the definition the world has taught you about being human, and into the spiritual truth of your being. The book of Genesis states that you are created in the image and likeness of God. The mundane is only the worldly experience, not who and what you truly are.

APPLICATION

Meditation is reaching in ... a meditation for you to begin:

> Holy Spirit walk with me,
> Inward through the annals of my past.
> I give you my fears.
> I give you my self-critical nature.
> I give you my blindness and denial.
>
> I was created in Divine Innocence.
> I seek my sense of innocence now.
> Knowing that I came to Earth to learn.
> I came to see my growth reflected in experience.
> I receive the gift of Christ consciousness.
> I came to give the gift of love.
>
> I see my actions as a cry for love.
> I see actions of others as a cry for love too.
> We all came here to learn.
>
> My task is to begin in this present moment,
> To give the gift of love again and again.
> I am not distracted by appearances.
> I look for and find ways to be loving.
>
> I keep my power and give my love.
> I keep my dignity and give my love.
> I keep my self-esteem and give my love.
> I keep my right discernment and give love.
> I honor my body and use it for only love.
>
> My power, dignity, self-esteem, discernment, and honor are the vessels of love out of which I give the love God pours through me into the world. Holy Spirit walk with me, in and through me, as me, as love. Amen.

CHAPTER TWENTY TWO

FINDING YOUR PURPOSE

Star light shining bright
Calling to my child's heart,
If I hope with all my might,
Will life give me a part?

A part to play, so special
That overcomes my fear.
My love bursts forth eternal,
To live that plan so dear.

Author

I believe we had a purpose in being born into this particular lifetime. We aren't just drifting aimlessly in the cosmos. Can we discern a life purpose, our own life purpose? Who or what set the purpose? Are we predetermined, predestined, or are we really free?

Some people have a real sense of what their purpose is, and some do not. Your purpose has been inside of you, calling to you throughout your life. It keeps showing up in little things. What do you love to do? What makes you tingle when you think of it? What do you wish you could get paid for doing? Where does your main talent lie? What are you good at, or even just wish you were good at? These are all questions that will help you discover it.

Aptitude tests may or may not be of assistance. You could be wonderful at working with people, but a childhood trauma has made you afraid. Secretly, you long to be a teacher, but an unfortunate childhood experience in school made you feel stupid. You have not overcome it and cannot allow yourself the joy of teaching.

Based upon a misperception of yourself, on an aptitude test, you may avoid affirmative answers to people or relationship questions. Perhaps a friend or acquaintance sees you in a different light and has reflected a beautiful perception of you. Did you turn it down flat, even though it stirred you inside?

Some people feel that God has a purpose, an individual purpose, for them. Is there something referred to as a calling? At one time I made the statement, "Here I am God, use me!" This would seem to point to an influence outside of ourselves, or "from above."

All of these refer to a summons from within you to express in your life the combination of talents which you possess. They are there to serve in your experiences as you interact with the world and learn to co-create with God. They are yours uniquely. They are truly your personal calling or purpose.

Ask deep within yourself to have your purpose revealed to you. Be persistent. It is important. We often have things so repressed that the purpose becomes buried under the heap. The good news is that you have help. The Divine Design within you knows the purpose and is constantly finding ways to reveal it to you. It manages to peek through the dense camouflage to signal you, to get your attention.

USE A VERB

Your purpose is best described in a verb, an action word. It has to do with serving others and serving the Divine Design: humanity unfolding in the likeness of God using the mirror of human experience. What can just one person do to help humanity to unfold, evolve, and spiritually progress? You are always an intricate part of the unfolding pattern. Without you, the universe is not complete. Without your part of the pattern, the tapestry lacks a thread that absolutely must be there. Look at a piece of cloth that has a pulled, broken, or is missing thread. You can spot the flaw immediately.

You are part of this design because you are a qualified participant. Billions of souls want to incarnate at this time, but the planet only holds so many at once. Only the most highly qualified souls for this particular time are admitted. You are here! You came here with an expanded soul, and capability to discover and carry out your purpose.

Now that you know what to look for, you can see you are not worthless. Your effect on the lives of others is important. Every act that overcomes a seeming barrier affects everyone else who is working on the same thing. We overcome not only for ourselves, but we also clear a way for others as well. Just as early explorers blazed the trail for those who would come later, in spirit we set up an energy that is available to those who come after us. So if you are overcoming fear, illness, poverty, etc., you are a trail blazer.

Jesus said, "I go so that the comforter will come to you." The comforter is the development of our own Christ Nature. He left us a legacy to do the things he did and even more. He created a battery of energy that we are all able to tap into. He overcame the adversary, the illusion of the power of physicality, in every area of life. Then he said, "I am the way …" I believe this is what he meant. We partake in the substance of his life in remembrance of who we are. We carry on this unfolding work and spread it to the entire population of the world.

> Dare Away
> River of light beside my path,
> Dare I step into your way.
> Commit my soul, my mind, my heart,
> Living you now, this holy day?
>
> The co-creator's span of life
> Forever in the here and now,
> Sending a tidal wave of love,
> Affirming my joyous vow.
>
> Author

HERE TO CREATE

We are here to create in the energy world, the pathways of empowerment whereby humanity may traverse and transcend. Each of us has a part in this. It is built, not of visible things, but of the invisible substance of God. The visible world we create around us is a mirror of how we are doing in the invisible. As we empower others, we share the energy paths of empowerment with everyone. As we clarify understanding, we direct the energy of clarity. Empowerment and clarity become more easily attainable, and others are then freed to work in other areas of creation.

Empowerment and clarification are two areas of possible purpose. Yours may be building, persisting, comforting, organizing, preserving, etc. As a clarifier you may be a writer, a guide, a teacher. What is your present job? What do you do for humanity? If your purpose is to organize, you might be an accountant, you might design day-timers, be an administrative assistant, or manufacture closet organizers. Your present job may be just right for you if you understand something about your purpose.

YOUR MESSAGE

Merely finding your purpose is not the end, but the beginning. It begins the formulation of your soul journey from awakening, to purpose, to message.

You have begun to awaken to your spiritual nature, or you probably would not be interested in this book. You may know the exact time of your spiritual realization or it may have been so gradual that you are not sure when it happened. Perhaps you were born awake. Many people are. In fact most people are, but the world conditions us very early in childhood ignore our spiritual nature.

Being born in the last few days of 1939, my strong sense of "otherness" was the feeling that I didn't belong here. I did not fit somehow. I suffered a lot of fear, anxiety, misunderstanding, and a sense of being an impostor ... as if my body and persona were a costume. Probably my greatest fear was that someone would find out. Now I realize that was not a bad thing. The shift from being a fearful child to a knowing spiritual adult is a great relief.

I went through several levels of discovering my purpose. We often start on the surface with vocation. We search through vocations for satisfaction. Mere achievements become inadequate and we begin to look for meaning. This leads to the searching of the depths of our being for purpose. Questions surface: Why am I here? Was I put here? Why was I born? Is what I have experienced so far all there is?

Once you begin to explore purpose and meaning, you can feel it working in you and in your expression of life. What will your message to the world be? What teaching will your life signify?

Jesus' message was carried forward in what became known as The Sermon on the Mount. A friend asked me what my "sermon on the mount" would be. I created one following the pattern that Jesus used, simple and clear. His word, according to the translation, was "blessed." The word that more clearly expresses my purpose and path is "transformed." So here it is:

* Transformed are we when we lust after God with all our heart, mind, and soul.

My purpose is not just to love God in some intellectual way, but to really get turned on in my whole being until it feels like a love affair. The Book of Solomon, Song of Songs, is about a love affair with God. God is in the feminine in that writing, being wooed by humanity.

*Transformed are we when we can see a perfect being coming forth in every person.

This doesn't mean we have to like or agree with everyone, or condone their behaviors. It means that we can see beyond appearances, personalities, behaviors, cultures, nationalities, race, and religion to the essence of divinity within every human being. We can be aware of that essence in prayer and through divine wisdom, even though we might have to restrain, incarcerate, divorce, or otherwise separate ourselves from them.

We can now see humanity in a great struggle to awaken and express their godlike nature. We can see all the twists and turns this struggle takes. We can see an evolutionary movement in humankind that spans eons of time. All this gives greater meaning to the moment.

* Transformed are we when we empower the good with attention, support, and action.

We must retrain ourselves to focus upon constructive goodness. Have you heard the saying, "One flea can worry a whole dog?" We let the one "flea," one slight or mishap, spoil our day, even though fifty wonderful things have happened as well. We let our attention be drawn in by what we don't want.

In our world it takes a lot to anchor the desirable in our lives. We have busy daily schedules making a living, dealing with family, home, and stuff that breaks down. Some days it seems to get the best of us and we let the most important things go by the wayside. We let go of prayer, meditation, volunteering, giving, and activity in organizations that are keeping the good available in our world.

> With all of our good,
> Spinning around us ablur,
> Somewhere is a pathway,
> A footing so sure.
>
> Stop the merry-go-round,
> Dismount from the ride,
> Sit down in the quiet,
> And sit down ... inside.
>
> There is nowhere to go,
> There is only to be,
> Where the soul can be quiet,
> As night on Galilee.
>
>   Author

* Transformed are we when our minds automatically center on the truth of being in every situation.

This happens when we constantly, spiritually interpret the events of our lives. This happens when some part of us always sees the greater picture. This is when we are conscious of interfacing with the divine in every earthly experience.

Jesus was telling us about this truth of being when he said, "I do this that your name be glorified." Everything he did and experienced was reflective of God in expression. You are automatically a channel for God energy, love, goodness, abundance, health, and joy wherever you are, should you choose to be conscious of it.

* Transformed are we when our constant prayer is a "thank you" that God is our Source, eternal and unlimited.

We can become so attuned with spiritual law that we don't have to ask for mere survival. Our "daily bread" is a given in the universe. There is no need to beg, for when we beg in our prayers we have slipped into doubt that God will sustain us. We affirm our abundant supply!

When we demonstrate the law of abundance, we ask for what will help us co-create divine experiences, new worlds, "going where no one has gone before."

* Transformed are we when we empower ourselves to be natural Christs on earth.

The Christ nature is already ours. We stop giving in to dishonoring, disempowering thoughts about ourselves. It is not a function of ego to stand tall in spirit, to speak spiritual truth, to see clearly, and to act upon spiritual guidance for our lives.

* Transformed are we when we openly co-create with God our next level of experience.

We act upon our heart's desire as if it were God's will. We must stop fearing God's disapproval. There is no such thing. There only our own ignorance that makes us act out of foolishness, fear, and hatred. God doesn't punish us, we do.

God's will for you is the highest and best desire of your heart. We have been taught that the will of God is something hidden, something we won't like. We call a lot of cruel things "God's will" that are simply the result of our own error ways and misunderstandings.

Pierre Teilhard de Chardin said that man is on the cutting edge of his own evolution. We choose to evolve. God, or the Omega, beckons us to constantly come up higher in consciousness. Jesus said that we are to sit in his throne with him

(Christ nature) just as he sits in the throne of the Father (Christ empowered). We need to get out of our self-manufactured fears and get on with it!

This is my "sermon on the mount," my credo, my message to the world. Try looking at the pattern of the be-attitudes and use them to help you write your own credo. What is it you really believe, are committed to, and will live out in all of your days upon the earth?

Remember to have patience with yourself. I was on this path twenty-five years before I came up with all of this. You do not develop overnight or at first blush of spiritual realization. It takes work, patience, time, dedication, curiosity, and joy to bring it to life in you.

> Remember to be gentle,
>   As the ship settles down,
>   Testing the moorings,
>   Touching the ground.
>
> Remember to be gentle,
>   When people react,
>   Questioning the newness,
>   Is their place still intact?
>
> Remember to be gentle,
>   Though strength be your way.
>   The presence within you,
>   Works the wonders this day.
>
> Remember to be gentle,
>   Through this difficult birth.
>   You know well the process,
>   That transforms the earth.
>
> Remember that God is gentle.

Author

I AM MY QUEST!

Finding my purpose was my quest. There is always more to know about purpose and how it is expressing through me. My ministry is to be my quest. Being a Unity minister isn't my job or career. It is what I am as an expression of my purpose. I think it, dream it, ingest it, speak it, breathe it, even struggle constantly to expand it.

Ministers are often asked about their life outside the ministry. We have events that take place outside of church with family and friends, but essentially we have no life outside of purpose and truth. It is all ministry in one form or another.

Continually being on purpose, on course, on target is complete congruence. Any time I am tempted to act other than on my purpose, the pain is immediately there to remind me to turn myself around. The yawning abyss of nothingness awaits outside of God and I know I don't want to travel that realm again. I know where home is! The Book of Revelation states, "You will be a pillar in the temple of my God; never shall you go out of it; and I will write on you the name of God ..." Revelation 3:12

How lovely it is to be on purpose, congruent, harmonious and in co-creatorship with God.

> Who gives me a God?
> Sets the path I now trod?
> Yet I know that I know,
> Because I am and I grow.
>
> Sweet spirit in me born,
> Long before Christmas morn.
> I was already divine
> On each path I called mine.
>
> God is who I am.
> I choose my God plan.
> It's my God I now give,
> It is God's life I now live.

Author

ACTIVITY

1. Find a verb that best describes your purpose. Clarifier, organizer, stabilizer, beautifier, etc.
2. Beginning with your chosen verb, write your own sermon on the mount. It becomes your credo of blessing as you expand your belief system to include

all humankind. All of our inner work eventually radiates outward and it is good to be in a blessing state of mind in regard to those around us.

Clarified are we ...   Preserved are we ...
Comforted are we ...   Healed are we ...
Stabilized are we ...   Beautiful are we ...

Then write a paragraph about your beliefs and about how your purpose happens when it is put into action.

CHAPTER TWENTY THREE

GETTING INTO HEAVEN

"The possibility of the new heaven and the new earth is wrapped up in every act of life."

Imelda Shanklin

Of course, the Bible is full of references to heaven. The explanations were in terms of what people could relate to at that time. Fully fifty percent of the references are in the Book of Matthew. In the thirteenth chapter, the disciples asked Jesus why he spoke to them in parables or stories. He said, "To you it has been given to know the secrets of the kingdom of heaven."

What was Jesus trying to tell us? How is spiritual interpretation connected with heaven and our ability to know the secrets of it?

When we become disciples of our own Christ nature, we are entering the realm of inner knowing. We are "given to know." We are given access to God Mind, to wisdom, and understanding. We access it through the mirror of human experience, through spiritually interpreting what we see, until we come face to face with the absolute truth of our being.

Heaven is the state of mind in which we can see our divinity in all facets of our living. Not just in the intellect, but in our experiences, our interactions, and our daily labors.

HEAVEN IS LIKE ...

—A man who sowed good seed in his field.
—Like a grain of mustard seed a man planted.
—Leaven a woman puts into flour and the whole loaf is affected.
—Treasure hidden that a person may find.

—A merchant in search of fine pearls.
—A net gathering fish of every kind.
—A householder who brings old and new out of his treasure.
—A king settling accounts with servants.
—A king who gave a marriage feast to his son.

Heaven is our life as active, fruitful, expansive, prosperous, searching, varied, time spanning, rewarding, and celebrating beings. You can see all these things in those descriptions.

Where is heaven? "At hand." "in the midst of you"
For how long? "It will not pass away."
What do I have to be like? Childlike, teachable, willing!

Jesus gave us lots of clues, all of them do-able and be-able. All of them are within reach of humanity when we come from that heavenly state of mind. We are made of the stuff of God and from the perfect pattern of God for humanity. "We are Heaven-made" according to songwriters, Carlos and Johnny.

HOW DID WE GET OUT OF HEAVEN?

In leaving the Garden of Eden, we left that dimension as purely spiritual beings and took on a physical nature in order to find heaven again through the dense nature of the physical. We came to Earth school to learn to create the heavenly state at this level, in order to qualify as co-creators with God.

Heaven is finding our happiness in everything we are and everything we are doing, regardless of the appearance or circumstance in which we find ourselves.

Happiness is a state of mind that we learn to choose. In growing up on planet Earth, we have learned that appearances can look real, threatening, and we can feel threatened and hurt by them. Thus, we have learned many defensive responses to these appearances:

| fear | anger | resistance | jealousy | guilt | blame |
| sorrow | angst | withdrawal | depression | attack | anguish |

Why no positive ones? Joy and happiness are often considered frivolous, accidental, fleeting, and naïve. So we often learn to value them least. Because life is hard, we tend to believe misery is the norm and joy is not. Most folks do not feel worthy of joy and have been taught not to feel worthy of heaven.

HOW DO WE STAY OUT OF HEAVEN?

We keep ourselves out of heaven by believing the threatening appearances are our reality. Our reality consists of what appears to us from the outside world. The *Course in Miracles* states that nothing that is real can be threatened because only what is of God is real. This is a tough lesson to internalize because the solid, three dimensional, material world is so dense that our bodies and lives can appear to be harmed by it.

We let the world define us, giving our experiences their meanings and their value. The world sets a standard for us, and teaches us to measure ourselves and our worth by its scale. If we happen to fit that scale most of the time, we may tend to agree with it. If, like me, you didn't quite qualify for the kudos on this scale, you wouldn't find success and happiness try as you might. I looked for another measure and/or alternative reality.

Some find another reality in insanity, crime, drugs, alcohol, abuse, gangs, and a variety of fanaticisms. None of those were my choice. My alternative to the material world is the world of Spirit, the world that Jesus found. I am not measured there, but loved. It was and is the kingdom of heaven.

HOW DO WE GET BACK IN?

Jesus taught us how and where to find the kingdom of heaven. The message was to stop looking to the outer world for your definition, your meaning, your happiness, and look to yourself. Look inside. The kingdom of heaven is within you.

Easier said than done! The intellectual ego-based mind has set up barriers to the inner realms with incessant chatter about the outside world. It is serving up truck loads of opinions, emotions, judgments, catch phrases, clever sayings, evasive maneuvers, hidden agendas, memories, and a litany of warnings and scare tactics.

It is like a Star Trek holodeck of images, sounds, and situations that fool the senses into thinking the terrors are real. We must get past this false information and insist upon realizing the truth of our nature instead.

We perhaps thought we already knew our true nature, mind, body, and emotions. We thought we were only physical beings that can somehow reason. We just have to be luckier and smarter than the next guy, and we'll make it. To where?

"For you say, 'I am rich. I have prospered. I need nothing;' not knowing that you are wretched, pitiable, poor, blind and naked!" *Revelation 3:17*

We must learn to really see. We must see past the images, past the litany and cacophony, to that part of us that stands apart and observes all of this. This is the part of us that has always known the truth and has awaited our return to sanity.

Maurice Nichol, in *The Work*, called it the observer self, that part of us that can reflect upon what we are doing. That part of us that can say, "See? There is Carole driving her car. See Carole get impatient with the driver that cut in front of her. Hear Carole tell him off, in her head of course! Interesting!"

What is that part of us that has observational powers? Who is it that speaks when the intellect is quiet? What is the feeling nature that is not the emotions?

When you have a feeling about something, it is not a physical emotion, but a sensing of something. Emotions are governed by our thoughts and can be changed by thoughts. Resentment can be changed to love through rational thought. The sensing or feeling comes from the influence of wisdom that comes from spirit. It is not subject to change nor is it under our mental control. We can only choose to listen to it or ignore it.

If we can observe our actions in a detached manner, can we also turn these observational powers inward toward the activity of God within us? I believe this is what spiritual interpretation is about. It is learning to observe all of life from a high place in consciousness.

The passage in *Revelation* 3:23 says, "To those who conquer, I will grant them to sit with me on my throne, as I myself conquered and sat down with my Father on his throne …"

Jesus also fought his way through this dense vibration of physical living, the temptations of the outer world, the engulfing emotions, and the fears of humankind, to be "about his Father's business." He sits on the throne of co-creatorship with God, and invites us to do the same.

FROM WORDS TO SILENCE

We verbally make our way into the non-verbal realm. We talk ourselves into that quiet place with words of encouragement, self-love, and appreciation. These words are not from the ego, but words about being a child of God, a creation of the Most High. Soon we find we are not speaking but silent. Words trail off into that quiet place within where we are in constant communion with God.

In arriving at the silence, we are on the threshold of discovering reality such as the outside world cannot comprehend. It is a vast inner world that is not empty, but full. It is full of the invisible substance out of which comes all life form. It is full of wisdom, power, and truth such as we can never experience from the material world.

From the silence we draw our life energy. We draw the pure untainted stuff of God into our realm of life experience that we form according to our imagination. We can only draw from the silence by arriving there ourselves.

NEVER COMING BACK

Life is progressive. We can move in leaps and bounds, or we can crawl at a snail's pace. Sometimes we try to hide, to go back to the land of three-dimensional thinking, but Spirit beckons us upward and onward. Once our thinking expands, we can't shrink it again. We can try, but the urging nags us at every turn and speaks to us in our dreams. We have flashes of insight unbidden and a restlessness in mind that continues to search despite our reluctance. Stepping over this spiritual threshold means we begin to walk in the fourth dimension, and we can never go back to the way we were.

You will find this in the archetypal description called "The Caves" in Plato's *Republic*. In this story, people are chained in a cave while facing the back wall. The only light comes from the mouth of the cave, and the people interpret life according to the distorted shadows on the cave wall. Then one person is taken from the cave into the light to see the truth, and is then returned to the cave and the shadows. Now they know the truth and the challenge of being returned to the world of shadows after experiencing the truth.

There is a certain amount of agony in seeing the truth initially, because we want to go out and save the world. We want to tell everyone we meet about the truth and the shadows, and only a few may listen. Such was the agony of Jesus. But the agony is nothing compared to the ecstasy of knowing the truth. In knowing the truth, we are free from the threat of fearful shadows. Now we can truly know joy!

HEAVEN IS

Heaven is knowing the truth of being that sets you free from unreasoning fear.

Heaven is basing your happiness upon the truth of your inner being where it is safely rooted.

Heaven is seeing the greater picture in everything you do, so that you aren't drawn into narrowness.

Heaven is receiving the learning and the gift from every experience you have so you can grow.

Heaven is knowing that nothing can touch you where you truly live. Not even disaster or death.

Heaven is having this knowledge for eternity, and being free to co-create with God wonderful worlds of experience without end.

Heaven is having joy be your predominant emotion and happiness your only chosen state of mind.

Heaven is knowing how to spiritually interpret your life and experiences, find the spiritual gift, seeing the constant evolution of your soul, and never be trapped in mental limitation again.

ADAM AND EVE

Adam and Eve were in heaven, the garden of Eden. They were beings in spirit only, who chose to eat from the tree of the knowledge of good and evil. They chose the course that would bring them ultimately into full co-creatorship with God.

In order to co-create with God, we must stand outside of heaven or divine order, and deal with the chaotic, unformed substance from which God created. We must learn to create according to Principle that which is patterned after God. We must learn to distinguish between what is God and what is not, what is eternal and what is not, thereby reconnecting with heaven.

We now realize that the light is never overcome by the darkness, no matter how small the flame or how vast the dark. We might put a light out for lack of fuel or attention, but it is never the darkness that puts it out. In spirit, we can withdraw ourselves from the light by turning away from the truth so easily that we think it has gone out. But when we turn back, it is still there. Scientists have discovered that we are never without light. There are a zillion bands of light, only a few of which humanity can perceive. Even though we cannot perceive the light because of our limitation, it is always here. God is always here.

Heaven always awaits us. It is at hand. It is in the midst of us. It will not pass away until all is accomplished. All we have to be is teachable, willing, and childlike in our openness. This is our task.

THE JOURNEY

Adam and Eve are the beginning of our journey home. We took a risk: We chose to leave heaven, or the haven of the garden of unconscious bliss, to become conscious co-creators with God. Experiencing the knowledge of good and evil, or the polarities of physical living, is the result of that choice.

We can look at this polarity as a continuum that stretches between opposite extremes: yes and no, yin and yang, light and dark, visible and invisible, good and evil. We live our lives moving back and forth between these poles, striving for balance somewhere in the middle. We are looking to live our lives in that harmonious place between two extremes.

When we move too far toward one extreme, our life experiences become difficult because they are lacking the proper weighting on each side. We find ourselves always fighting imbalance, compensating, as if we were walking on a slanted sidewalk. The strain of imbalance takes up our energy and causes unnatural alignment of body, mind and emotions.

Don't confuse this with boring middle-of-the-road living, where we take no risks. Rather, it is the artful challenge of a balance beam walker. Our life journey after leaving the Garden of Eden is a process of developing our faculties from infancy (the wobbly toddler), to adulthood (choosing the balance), to Christhood (being the balance).

The Old Testament is symbolic of our psychological development as human beings. The events give us a road map of that level of development. The violence and difficulties of the Old Testament people are a mirror of the intricate workings of our psychological development. For an in-depth study of characters of the Old Testament, and what they represent within you, refer to Unity's *Metaphysical Bible Dictionary*.

The New Testament is about our spiritual development and the spiritualizing of all we have accomplished in consciousness. Our spiritual nature, symbolized by the characters in the Gospels, lifts us up and takes us the rest of the way home.

We must accomplish our spiritual development sufficiently in order to co-create with God. Jesus was the greatest risk taker. He could have remained in the quiet life of a teacher, revealing himself to only a select few. This is what mystical teachers of his time and before him did. Mystery schools were for the select few, those who had to go through years of training and initiation before they were allowed into the study of the actual mysteries. The tests they had to pass were incredibly rigorous and required excellence of the students to even physically and mentally survive.

But Jesus revealed himself as an agent of God, that we might find our own divine relationship with God. He did not explain the quantum physics of the miracles he performed, nor put people through difficult tests. He gave them the leaven that would expand their living through story-telling and parables, so they would find the pathway naturally by living his teachings.

This exercise will assist you in clearing up the areas of your life that still bring you pain or unhappiness. So long as we live on this planet, we will always have some housekeeping to do. Events come along that we inadvertently allow into our experience as pain and it is good to have a way to neutralize their effect.

ACTIVITY

1. What areas of your life are not yet heavenly? List them carefully in your notebook.

2. Write down steps you can take in your thinking to create a more heavenly state of mind about them. In other words, you can neutralize negative feelings with affirmative thoughts, and begin constructive ways of dealing with the unheavenly state. Visualize how you would like things to be good for all concerned, and match that with thoughts that would produce it.

3. How will you take action accordingly? It helps to write this down, too, so you have a plan on paper. Then you can see it more clearly, modify where necessary, and have a good reminder when you need it. You may have to test your plan several times to get the result you desire.

CHAPTER TWENTY FOUR

ASKING FOR THE PLAN

"Do not beg in your prayers, but praise and give thanks for the new self-manifesting God of abundance fulfilling every desire of your heart."

Charles & Cora Fillmore: *Teach Us To Pray*

As a child, I thought that everyone knew the plan but me. Embarrassed, I didn't ask. I really didn't know what to ask. I felt that I had been left out of something very important, and I didn't want anyone to know. How did others get the plan and not me? Something was missing for me.

Being the baby of the family, I didn't figure out that everyone I knew was older and had more years of experience. A high school art teacher gave me my first clue when he said that the seniors often did better in art because they had seen more than the younger students. Bingo! The light of understanding came on!

In my misunderstanding of religion, it seemed that I shouldn't have the audacity to ask about the big stuff either. Another light came on after my first divorce when my mother asked me if I had thought to ask God before I married. I was more than a little embarrassed because it had not crossed my mind. Asking God to know something I had no way of knowing wasn't in my awareness at all.

How does this asking take place? Contrary to popular belief, asking is not begging, beseeching, bargaining, or groveling. It is claiming. Claiming? Yes! Claiming what God has for you. It is "God's good pleasure to give to you the kingdom" and all Godly wisdom. It is yours for the asking.

Over the years of my unfoldment, I have learned to ask and ask. O.K., God, what is happening here? What do I need to know, do, or say? Where are my keys? Ask everything! Our job is to ask for guidance and to choose guided steps. This is the tool that gets us to the mountain. Ask where the mountain is and then make every step you take go in that direction. It is only possible if you ask.

Do I actually expect an answer to every silly question I have? Yes. No question is too silly or trivial to ask God, and I expect an answer in complete detail. Make no mistake, I do not ask God in a insincere way. We are open to receive only what we expect and respect. God can only answer through us, and our expectation is the opened door. It took me a few years to shed the King James language and use plain talk. I really didn't want answers in cryptic Olde Englishe, so why ask my questions in it? You know, the thees and thous, and cansts and willsts? I hear people launch into this antiquated language when leading public prayer and it always jolts me. God is now. We should be in the now with God. God is real. We can be real with God. God is clear. We need to be clear. God is in everything. We can ask everything. God hears in our own tongue, in the language of our hearts, and answers accordingly. We don't need to suddenly cover up who we really are with something unnatural to us.

WHY NOT BEG?

Begging and beseeching are forms of doubt and fear. We fear that God won't give us what we ask, or worse, we don't want to appear arrogant. We think God can be flattered if we grovel or persuaded if we nag. How ghastly for God, after creating us out of the very God stuff. We were promised that if we asked, we would receive. How ungrateful and unbelieving of us to ignore that heritage and not ask, treating the promise as if it were a lie.

Jesus told us to follow him. In other words, follow his example. At the tomb of Lazarus he said, "Thank you Father that you hear me and I know you hear me always!" John 11:41-42. He didn't say, "Please, please God make this work so I won't look like a fool in front of all these people!"

We must get over our lack of self-esteem and confidence in co-creating with God in this planetary experience. We must take hold of the reality of our true partnership with God, our inherent Christ nature.

ARE WE ARROGANT?

Arrogance is believing that we set the tone or reality of the relationship, and not God. Arrogance is taking license in our fear-ridden ego mind to reinterpret that beautiful relationship into one of fear. Arrogance is spreading that poison or fear among our brothers and sisters all over the world. We are seeing today the results of that arrogance. It is an unnatural posture that manifests aberrant behaviors resulting in violence and cruelty. People cower and tremble before a terrifying image of God, and then do violence to themselves and others as a result. Fear becomes impotence, then anger and rage, and then violence. Fear separates us from the source of life, and the result is death in soul and spiritual understanding.

HOW SHOULD WE ASK?

How do *you* want to be asked for something? How do *you* want to be approached for love, help, friendship, or partnership?

I want a friendly, straightforward, and confident approach. I want to see a person approach me out of self-knowledge and self-esteem. I enjoy someone who knows truly who they are and who I am, spiritually, at least. How about being light hearted, honest, open, and enthusiastic? It is clean and clear, and genuinely healthy.

Often I sit down companionably with my God. We share the fun and excitement of getting together as me. I place before the Divine within me my heart's desire, my latest pet project, my needs, questions, and my certainty of a good result. No games. It is the most wonderful and productive of relationships.

Jesus could not work through the hysterics of the Syro-Phoenician woman who wanted her daughter to be healed. She was begging and wailing constantly all day, and the disciples in their frustration asked Jesus to send her away. He jolted her out of her hysteria with an insult, referring to her as a dog. Suddenly realizing that she wasn't going to accomplish her goal in this manner, she turned from wailing to intelligent humility and reason. She answered saying that the dogs are happy to pick up the crumbs under the table of the Children of Israel. Because of her changed state of mind, Jesus could now heal her daughter through her and did so.

ATTITUDE IS ALL

Our attitude is controlled by our beliefs about life, ourselves, and God. I know there are many ideals presented to you. Often people say, "I would like to be like him/her, so calm and unruffled." We try willpower, shame, or guilt in imitating another's response to God. Force or imitation will not work. It is your belief that makes the difference, always.

If you believe people are inherently good, what will your attitude be when people approach you? It will be positive.

If you believe God is in your corner, ready to bestow all good upon you, what will your attitude be toward prayer? It will be affirmative.

If you believe that life is a benign school and you a precious student, what will your attitude be toward all events in your life? It will be adventurous.

If you believe that your predominant thinking determines your life experiences, what will your attitude be toward training your mind? It will be eager.

If you believe that a part of yourself is in every driver on the highway, what will be your attitude as you drive? It will be gracious.

If you have a less than good attitude in general, begin by searching out what you basically believe about things such as:

Money	Marriage	Decisions
People	Gangs	Drivers
War	Romance	Divorce

You can list more. If you want a great attitude you need a great belief.

ASKING IS CLAIMING

Have you heard about staking a claim in the gold rush days? Have you heard about homesteading on the prairie? You staked out a piece of land, lived on it and worked the acreage for a specified period of time, and it became yours. You were granted title to it.

Asking God is equivalent to staking a claim for what you want. You claim a certain field of thought, you occupy it, live in it and work it until it becomes your own. If there is something you want in your life, you must have the consciousness for it before you can have title to it. That means you fully occupy it in your thoughts, explore every facet of it, work it, plant it, cultivate it, and harvest it. It then becomes your reality, your experience.

This is a long process or a short one, depending upon how deep the roots of certain of your beliefs are concerning life. If illness or poverty has been your experience since childhood, and also your family's, the roots will be deep and more patience will be required for manifestation of healing or abundance.

Myrtle Fillmore, co-founder of Unity, discovered the power of affirmative prayer while searching for a way to heal herself of life-threatening Tuberculosis. She began to affirm the health of every cell in the body. Believing she was a child of God, and could not inherit illness, she lifted those cells from the effects of her error thinking to their original perfection.

Silent Unity is the twenty-four hour prayer service that resulted from Myrtle Fillmore's discovery of affirmative prayer. People began to pray with her in this new affirmative fashion. The results began to pour in through personal letters.

People were healed, prospered, guided, and their lives were transformed. We call it scientific prayer because it has been researched and the results of positive prayer are found to be dependable attested to by the correspondence received reporting results after prayer has been requested. More information about these successes can be attained by contacting Silent Unity at Unity School of Christianity, Unity Village, Missouri. The affirmation of the perfection of our being, and the alignment of our whole mind and heart with that affirmation brings results. God is reliable. Spiritual law is reliable. Human beings must train their minds and hearts to be reliable in alignment with the truth.

As human beings we are prone to waver back and forth between faith and doubt. We ask in faith and the answer is on its way. We shift into doubt before the answer reaches us and place ourselves out of range to receive it. How often to we call upon God, ask the question, and hang up the receiver before we get the answer? The answer always comes. In order to be on hand to receive we must be in the same place in consciousness as when we asked.

Our task is to train the mind to stay on frequency and not wander. We need to train the mind to stay in affirmation of the good, and not be persuaded to doubt that we deserve it, or that it will come. You become persuaded by your belief about the area that your prayer is focused upon. If you believe poverty is your lot, it will be hard to stay on track with prosperity thoughts, because appearances of lack will snatch you away. The first time your wallet is empty, a negative ego voice will say, "See? See? I told you that it wouldn't work for you!" And you will fall into poverty thinking again.

This exercise has to do with training the mind. It is more detailed than the previous exercise and will give you more information to work with. We have so many hidden beliefs that were given to us as children. They often come from the overarching mythology of a society and are not necessarily written anywhere. They are considered common knowledge. Everybody knows it! Unfortunately much of it is not true, born of hardship, and subsequently believed.

ACTIVITY

1. List some issues in your life and assess their depth. We will take time as an example. We'll put time in the "Issue" column and list the attitude we have toward time in the "Attitude" column. Underneath this attitude is a belief or assumption about time. It would look something like this:

Issue	Attitude	Belief
Time	Impatient	There is never enough
Time	Rushing	Time is fleeting
Time	Frightened	There is too much to do
Time	Desperate	I'll never catch up
Time	Bored	Too much time is bad

Once you know your beliefs and how you presently respond to them, you can change them. This is how you change them into something helpful and useful. We will list the belief from the above under "Time" and write an affirmation that we will place under "New Belief." The new belief is the affirmation that you will take with you and thoughtfully repeat from time to time throughout your day. The idea is to replace the old limiting belief in subconscious mind with the new one. It takes about thirty days of concentrated effort. The subconscious mind contains your thought habits and they do not change on a whim. You need to convince subconscious mind that you are serious and are not going to give up.

Time	New Belief
Never enough	God gives me all the time I need.
Fleeting	I slow down and time slows down.
Too much to do	I prioritize my tasks and God easily accomplishes all through me.
Never catch up	I am in command and I set the pace.
Too much is bad	Time is precious, and I use it for working, thinking, relaxing and praying. Time is exciting!

Try another one:

Issue	Attitude	Belief
Money	Fearful	I can't hang on to money
Money	Hate	A big struggle to get any
Money	Confused	Too complicated
Money	Distain	Filthy lucre

Money is a tough one for most people. We have so many conflicting ideas about it. But money is spiritual currency in physical form. It responds to those who respect and care for it, and runs away from those who misunderstand and misuse it. It hates to be wasted and goes where it grows.

Money	New Belief
Fear of losing it	I am divinely guided to handle all my funds. They are mine to keep or disburse as God directs.
Struggle to get it	I do what I love and the money flows into my life and accounts. I am prospered in all that I do.
Too Complicated	I understand clearly and easily all that concerns my finances.
Filthy Lucre	Money is spirit-made currency in all my affairs. It is a gift of God and I honor it in all that I do.

You can do this exercise with other things in your life such as relationships and career. Any area in your life that needs upgrading will benefit by this.

Remember to write down and take with you only your new beliefs and discard the old ones. Read the new beliefs over with excitement and expectancy. Watch for the changes in your life and give thanks for each one, great or small. Make it a habit to think in this new way, and have fun doing it.

CHAPTER TWENTY FIVE

WHAT IS YOUR PART IN THE GREATER PICTURE?

"As a Being of Light, you have free passage wherever in God's Universe your particular consciousness will allow …"

Emmanuel's Book

Many people in the sixties experimented with LSD, and tore the curtain of intellect, as the curtain of the Temple was torn at Jesus' crucifixion. Some of those who used the drugs, in stepping into the next realm so suddenly and without proper preparation, did some permanent damage to the functioning of their finite minds. Such powerful indelible images upon an unprepared mind caused flashbacks and sometimes insanity.

The way to understanding your part is always to begin with asking. Always ask in a prayer state of mind for the next step. Ask in an openness to hear and to comprehend. Ask in a state of confidence, curiosity, joy, anticipation, and utmost respect.

It may be helpful to create a divine space for yourself in a quiet comfortable meditation place. Quiet meditation music and soft lights help. You may have heard all of this before, and you may have experienced guided meditation already.

I use the word "may" because I'm not convinced that absolute comfort is necessary. Some people are in constant pain and can still do this work. Jesus did not have a meditation room. In fact, he went into the wilderness, stressing his body with fasting, heat, and sun for long periods of time. He created an altered state of consciousness with deprivation and discomfort, and still communicated with God. How did he do this without incurring injury or death? Preparation. His preparation was mental, emotional, and spiritual alignment.

So if you are not accustomed to the more severe environment that Jesus chose, you might start with a more comfortable, private, and peaceful place. Do what works best for you to help you concentrate and not be distracted.

FIRST, STRETCHING EXERCISES

It sounds like a preparation for a physical workout, doesn't it? Well this is preparation for a mental workout. The key is a prepared mind. Begin to stretch the mind a little beyond its usual realm of ideas. Start looking around at other philosophies, religious thinking, and search out the root spiritual principles. This is simply to enlarge the framework of your mind to include many points of view as valid along with yours. Become comfortable with paradoxical thinking.

A paradox is a statement that is seemingly self-contradictory, an argument that arrives at opposite conclusions, seemingly equally valid. For example:

1. We kill for peace and defend life with killing.
2. The more we find solutions to our problems, the more problems seem to be spawned by those solutions.
3. Chemotherapy saves life by destroying living cells.
4. God's command was "Thou shall not kill," yet God commanded Joshua to kill everyone in the promised land.
5. Jesus died that he might defeat death.
6. We prosper by giving and tithing.

These all seem like contradictions unless they are understood at the level of spiritual principle. We raise the paradox to the spiritual through spiritual interpretation. Since creation is abundance, the Principle is abundance, and in giving money away we create a vacuum so that prosperity can rush in.

The Zen masters used the Koan as a tool for their students to learn this higher way. "What is the sound of one hand clapping?" The answer can only be demonstrated by the clapping motion with only one hand. If you speak the word "silence" then you haven't risen above the paradox. You must BE silent.

If we are to be healed, we must know the process. The answer to the physical is found at the emotional level. It is our negative emotions that depress the immune system and open the body to disease. So we must change the emotion.

The answer to the emotional problem is found at the mental level. We change thinking in order to change emotions. The answer to any mental confusion is found in the spiritual. In order to change our thinking we must consult spiritual wisdom in prayer.

Each level may be paradoxical to itself, but it becomes clear and makes perfect sense in the next. If you are ill in body, you look to the emotional state for healing. If the feelings are negative and harmful, you look to the metal state to heal the emotional nature, in order to heal the body. If your mental state is negative you go to the spiritual to heal your mind, which heals your emotions, which heals the body.

Expanding the mind is so important. If your mind runs in only one channel of thought, it is too limited. I remember when television was first marketed. I remember the first TV set in my Ohio neighborhood. A bunch of us kids piled into the neighbor's living room to watch a snowy Fred Waring Show. I was amazed when I visited my grandmother in New Jersey that she could get six channels. Wow! We got only one in semi-rural Ohio. Now we are looking at hundreds of channels. So it is with the mind. We must expand our repertoire of thoughts and choices. We must have an infinite variety of combinations of ideas. We must push out the walls of limited thinking and live comfortably with ever increasing choices. God is still your "search engine" and will help you find the right choices for you.

START BY STRETCHING SELF-IMAGE

Perhaps you have been taught to be modest, and not to make too much of yourself. You have kept your fantasies hidden. You are the princess, the prince, the hero of every mental fantasy episode. Secretly, of course.

There is a story about the infant child of a king that was hidden among the peasants to protect him from the king's enemies. The child grows up not knowing he is a prince. He lives as a peasant until one day the truth is revealed, and he learns that he has a kingdom to rule.

It is legitimate to identify with the hero in movies because Hollywood expects us to identify. The hero parts are written for that reason. We have tears, smiles, exhilaration, but only for the duration of the movie. Then the fantasies go underground again, to be savored in moments of reverie when we are alone.

Allow me to give you permission to actively and deliberately incorporate your hero fantasy into your spiritual reality. You have those fantasies because the hero part of you is longing to express. (The word hero is also feminine, coming from the goddess Hera.)

Many times in guided meditation a group of us have been instructed by the leader to ask the question, "Who am I?" The question has to do with the truth of being, not early family or worldly position. One of my answers came through like this:

> I am the seer. I am always in the same high place, surveying creation, events and experiences.
>
> I am in the world, but not spiritually of it.
>
> I am the mother creator/healer that births and cares for all manner of manifestation in my life.
>
> I am the chooser of what will have life in me and what will not. What will manifest as my experience.
>
> My conscious attention is an empowering light and force that sets into motion a lifetime that is the reflection of my true being.

Without the expanded mind, and knowledge of the fourth dimension, this sounds like pure arrogance and foolishness. But at the spiritual level, it is much closer to the truth than all of our physical identities.

When something like this comes through a meditation, it is a message from the divine nature that we are to use for further contemplation of who we are. It is the template against which we build our future experiences.

The first part of the answer reminds me to be the observer, to look at events from a greater perspective. It reminds me to stay above the snares of the intellectual and emotional world, the realm of ego and it's empty values.

The second part reminds me of the birthing function at the next level that embodies my vision of life. Everything comes from within. Everything in form and experience in my life originates in the invisible within me.

The third part reminds me of the power that I have been given as part of my creation. It reminds me that what I focus my mind upon becomes my experience. That wherever I am in consciousness, and whatever is contained in my thoughts, sets in motion my life.

WHO IS IN CHARGE OF THE PICTURE

The evolutionary direction of my life and consciousness is designed by me. God in me waits to see what I will choose, and empowers whatever I decree by my predominant thinking. It doesn't matter whether it is good for me or not. God doesn't recognize human good or bad. God doesn't make my choices for me. God simply answers when I knock and opens the door to whatever I choose.

When I expand my mind and my self-concept, and then choose the highest and best that my mind can imagine and articulate, I begin to live the greater picture. The more I live the greater picture, the more expanded my consciousness becomes. This is where limitlessness resides. Your awareness and your experience spiral upward together.

We are unlimited. We can have whatever we want, but we have to be able to choose it with the majority of our whole being. We have to be expanded enough to encompass the greater realm in our thinking.

If you want a castle, you have to be able to walk the halls in consciousness first, feel it as yours, hear the echoes of your footsteps as you walk, smell the odors and consciously be the resident with all that it requires. Now if you know nothing about castles and large spaces make you nervous, echoes in the night are scary to you, you have some work to do … or maybe you will find that you don't really want a castle at all.

By the way, don't forget the prosperity consciousness that goes with it. We can pick out an item like a castle and perhaps manifest it in our lives, but it won't stay there without everything else in place. It could become a terrible burden and that would be ruinous to our present life. God created a whole universe with everything working in concert, not just a lot of items working independently. A movie director sees the whole movie. A car manufacturer can see the whole transportation picture, not just the wheels or paint job.

THINK BIG!

If I were going to be the director of creating a new civilization on another planet and could take any two people in history with me, it would be Gene Roddenberry and Walt Disney. They developed the kind of world I love to participate in … worlds full of adventure, goodness, love, beauty, gentleness, action, wholesomeness, and infinite possibility. Their worlds were inclusive and full of variety. So often when it seemed that they had thought of everything, they went on to create more, bigger, and better again.

In essence, they are my true partners in complete worlds, and others like them. In a moment of asking for a description of true partnership, this poem came through:

> I love an adventurous man,
> Who does not have a sensible plan;

> Who is open to Spirit,
> And too smart to fear it!
> He exists as I AM and I CAN!
>
> Author

Actually, we are creating our world all the time. If we work on it as diligently and carefully as Roddenberry and Disney, we can have a marvelous experience. It takes:

1. An overall idea of the kind of world we want.
2. Describing the cast of characters.
3. Envisioning the setting.
4. An overall sense of the story line.
5. Writing and editing the script over and over.
6. Shooting or imaging the scenes.
7. Being true to Principle as we formulate the process.
8. Keeping it moving toward the ideal.
9. Incorporating the prosperity Principle to support it.

Perhaps you had not considered the possibility of creating your world because it looked very much like everything had already been set up for you since childhood. Before you begin your own creation, you are experiencing your part in the scenes created by others for their lives. You are an actor in someone else's play until you begin to write your own.

"As A Man Thinketh In His Heart, So Is He"

What does thinking in your heart mean? It is creating from the center most part of yourself, that place where the Holy Spirit dwells. As you turn inward and call upon your spiritual nature to reveal the ideas, you will begin to know what that is. Thinking in your heart is a non-linear, non-intellectual activity. It is opening to the influx of spiritual wisdom and grace.

Does this sound like gobbledegook? It is, until you try it. To paraphrase an old saying, to those who have experienced it no explanation is necessary. To those who have not tried it, no explanation is possible. So try it. This is not a book of answers, but of direction indicators.

Great strides are being made by the Heartmath Research people in understanding the vibration of the heart as the most powerful within us. Heartmath is an innovative research organization that can be reached at HeartMath LLC, 14700 West Park Avenue, Boulder Creek, California 95006. The vibration of the intellectual mind is not as strong as the vibration of the heart. So they recommend that meditation be focused upon the heart, rather than the intellect, as a way of drawing answers.

WHAT IS YOUR THEME?

Here we go again! What theme runs in your heart? What has been your deepest longing? What speaks to you from everywhere as goodness? What always causes your soul to light up? What makes you sit up and take notice?

This way of questioning always leads us inward to our own truth. Answers to them emerge from you, not from books or others. I would be trespassing to presume to give you answers that can come only from you. I only know what comes out of me. These questions came out of the guiding nudges that I finally learned to listen to and value.

It is fun to learn to interpret these questions, urgings, and other things that happen around you. At first I got excited about parallel realities, or what appeared to be coincidences. These are things that happen in parallel, yet don't seem to be connected, or are separated by centuries. These events always light up my mind and curiosity. One time on the news I heard that our Secretary of State was going to the Kremlin in a camper because of the bugging problem in the embassy buildings. I could see the secretary riding through the gates of the Kremlin in this little camper vehicle, sort of like Jesus riding through the gates of Jerusalem on a little donkey. Each one portended a turning point in the history of mankind. I chose to make that connection instead of passing it off as frivolous.

I really believe that true spiritual power is found in being able to see to the heart of things, to interpret what is happening around me, seeing a deeper meaning than what appears on the surface. It gives me a sense of being able to see more of the universal of life and to extend myself through that understanding into being more universal myself. It has given me the ability to speak on Sunday mornings to a crowd of people and have them say that I touched them individually. They commented on how I touched on what they were experiencing at that very time, and asked me how I knew. The Universal does that, and I am incredibly gratified that it comes through me to touch the lives of others so helpfully.

My theme has come to be the empowering of each individual that I meet. Each person is here to achieve their full potential for good in the world, and this is one of the ways I can help. I love stories of empowerment, of women coming into their own, of the ghetto kid rising to prominence, of the bikers who help children, etc.

"Rags to riches" has been an important theme in American culture and literature. Physical rags to merely physical riches is the lower vibrational level of the story being told. The spiritual level that sings in my heart has to do with the ragged physical level of thinking that impoverishes the soul. People are transformed by spiritual awareness and spiritual thinking that enriches the soul. In this way they are forever prospered. Jesus told the woman at the well that if she drank of the water he would pour out for her, she would never thirst again. This is the water of spirit, the universal truth.

My life theme is to empower people to step into their spiritual life and awareness. People eventually come to the question in their material living, "Is this all there is?" The physical/psychological world no longer spurs them on to greater material achievement. Worldly success no longer satisfies. The myth of Sisyphus comes to mind, where he is doomed to push a huge stone up a hill only to have it roll down again and again. If we stay in the physical level of living only, we are subjected to this as well.

When we hit the wall, so to speak, if we ask the right questions, we save ourselves from being doomed to roll that stone up the hill over and over. Jesus, at the age of twelve, began to "be about his Father's business," his spiritual life. A cycle is completed and we must move upward in our perception of who we are. We must begin to manifest the divine, the Christ nature in us as us.

There are many stories that reveal how this is done. A few of these are the search for the Holy Grail, Jason and the Golden Fleece, Parsifal and the healing of the King's wound. These are all stories of how the incomplete physical nature must complete itself in a quest for its divinity. The search is inward, battling and overcoming the enemy fear, and claiming the prize. Jung called it the hero's journey. We are here to complete ourselves by identifying our true path, challenging the dragon of fear, and gaining our wholeness.

The dragons I have faced along the way are fear of confrontation, fear of rejection, fear of being deceived or appearing a fool, abandonment, and being found wanting in some essential ingredient. Are any of these familiar to you? I think they are pretty universal. Remember that these dragons are illusions created by the mind, and are harmful only to those who believe in them. We injure ourselves almost to the death of our self-valuing, until we conquer them.

The dragons are also our friends. They tell us what we must overcome in our error thinking. They are the signposts in our quest for wholeness. Do not make the mistake of thinking your challenges are bad or shameful. They may not be pleasant, but they point to the shortest path to the prize.

Recognizing Help

There are many triumphs along the way. We gather helpers, wizards, and lovers that are part of our success. We cannot complete this quest alone. Some of the helpers are the most unlikely that we could imagine. They are unlikely because they are the homely and crippled parts of ourselves that step forth at a crucial moment, to be our strength.

The wizards are those magical moments that transport us through seeming impenetrable barriers. The lovers are glimpses of God that attract us to our own ecstasy, our eventual union with the Divine. Too often we are disappointed when we mistake lovers for God instead of the glimpse that the feeling represents.

If you learn to spiritually interpret your life, you will see things from a higher perspective and not get lost or stuck in appearances, or mired in the journey itself.

Leap of Faith

Inevitably, in our story there comes a leap of faith. We take it when all avenues to the prize seem to evaporate, when it appears that we must take some suicidal leap into the unknown or quit. It simply means that our physical and psychological natures have taken us as far as they can, and we must allow a new vehicle to take over.

An unknown poet wrote that when we take that leap, we must assume that we will be given a landing place or be taught to fly. As we close our eyes, draw a deep breath, and take the leap, we awaken to find ourselves safe upon a new earth, and the prize of the new heaven is twinkling in the palm of our hand, shining in the heart.

This is the theme of our journey, and we will take many mini-journeys throughout the great journey. The prize is God, the power to set everything right, to vanquish all evil, and to bring peace and happiness to the ultimate kingdom, our INNER kingdom.

The greater picture is revealed to you continually as you become the owner of the prize. So long as you strive to maintain a Christ-like consciousness of God and manifest it in your life, the picture will eternally unfold in you.

The Bible says you will go from Glory to Glory, being transfigured over and over as you move ever toward living the Christ pattern within you. The Apostle Paul called it "growing up into the head of Christ." It means maturing in your Christhood, maturing in your understanding of God manifesting as you.

ACTIVITY

These exercises will simply help you stretch your perceptions. Unlimited ability to perceive greater and greater meanings and concepts is your goal. Don't feel defeated by them if you do not come up with definitive answers. Keep your thinking open to inspiration.

1. What are your paradoxes? Add to those I have listed in this chapter with some from your own life experiences.
2. Think of them from the perspective of Principle:
   a. Life and death. Life has no opposite.
      Birth and death are opposites.
   b. Giving and paying. Giving and tithing are a
      Principle in that as you give so you receive, even
      to overflowing. Paying is a duty at the physical
      level, an activity of even exchange.
3. Go into meditation and ask the question, "Who Am I?" Write down anything that comes to you regardless of how bizarre it might seem. To understand what your answer might mean, go to Principle to see it clearly. You are a child of the Most High, made of God stuff!
4. Write down some themes you think fit your life according to the subheading, "What Is Your Theme?" What do you see as the main theme of your life?

CHAPTER TWENTY SIX

FINDING GOD OR THE GLASS CEILING

> "For now we see in a mirror dimly, but then face to face. Now I know in part; then I shall understand fully, even as I have been fully understood."
>
> I Corinthians 13:12

Some are born with it, some learn it, and some find it by accident or trauma. Some open to it in a special ceremony, and some never have a clue.

What is IT? That's a good question. It is the question we came into this lifetime to answer. Some say that God chooses whom He/She will touch with understanding. They say that until you are chosen, you can't force it. Robert Browning calls it the imprisoned splendor, the light from within. Jesus called it the Father within.

We must have eyes to see the Presence of God, and ears to hear the special call. We must be developed in consciousness to the point that the appearance of the Holy Spirit is perceivable by us. Then we will just know without explanation.

Finding God is an individual pathway, where one seems to study and struggle and not find, and another simply awakens to it with no apparent effort. Finding God is a matter of grace, not subject to our earthly rules of fairness.

UNIVERSALITY

We have the opportunity to develop universal consciousness through use of the Universal Mind. In other words we develop our godlikeness by using God Mind instead of ego mind. Through it we can see the greater picture. We see humanity as a body of students moving through lessons or experiences. We can harbor hatred for none because we know the truth about them. We can be in situations but not identify with them, because we know the situation is an experience with a gift that they must look for. We can be in the midst of a way and somehow understand in a higher way.

How do we develop universal consciousness? Study. Keep the mind directed toward it. Pray about it. Ask for it. Make it the focus of your thinking. Be willing to give up all your usual responses to situations, and willing to see things in a new and larger way.

Be willing to have people misunderstand you. Don't be surprised when Jesus' words come true. "Blessed are you when men revile you and persecute you, and utter all kinds of evil against you falsely on my account." Matt. 5:11

The key to peace of mind in the midst of turmoil is to seek only to understand. So you don't need to seek to be understood. You are already understood. You are individually and universally known to God.

THE GLASS CEILING

As one who lives in fourth dimensional consciousness, who lives according to spiritual law, you will be different. Your light of truth will shine so brightly that the darkness in others will begin to howl.

Those you would introduce to spirituality and mentor along their way may turn upon you and revile you, because they have hit their glass ceiling. They cannot go beyond what they have earned in consciousness. They see dimly what they have not yet been able to fully attain and they fear their own inadequacies. They may turn and rend you, blame you, and it will be baffling to you because you have striven to do only good. But stay in spirit and you will grow to understand what is really happening.

The glass ceiling is that gate of passage that keeps the ego-centered mind from entering the Universal realms. If you look at the glass and see only the image of yourself, you cannot pass through. If you see God, *truly* see God, the way opens wide and you are most welcome.

Fear Is Separation

People who look into the glass and see only themselves still have work to do on their own consciousness, and are frustrated because they don't as yet have what you have. They can see through the glass darkly. Their fear takes over and they may find fault with you as an excuse to remove themselves from your light.

If you are a beginner on the path and are feeling anger against your mentor and teacher, think where this anger comes from in you rather than attack yourself or the mentor. What piece in you is missing that you are having difficulty finding. You will be tempted to blame others because your ego wants to survive and be your God. As the Christ comes forth in you, the Judas nature must die and it will put up a fight. We may approach this gate of passage over and over, until we finally are in the consciousness to overcome the ego, to truly see God, and pass on through it.

FINDING GOD

Finding God is more than believing in the theory of God within. It is more than agreeing with the theology that the second coming of Christ is within you and every other person. It is more than faith. It is the experience of knowing and honoring that which comes from deep within, something that is greater than your own logic and intellect.

From Believing To Knowing

Carl Jung was asked if after all he had suffered and learned, did he still believe in God. He said that he "no longer believed, he now knew." (Interview with Bill Moyers) He no longer experienced the precursor known as belief, but now possessed the full and complete knowing. God becomes our experience as us. God lives in us as us.

Again, remember, "To those who believe, no explanation is necessary; to those who do not believe, no explanation is possible." I know that if you are already immersed in that experience, my struggle to explain isn't necessary. But for those who believe, but still do not have the experience, I will continue to try to put words around it.

You find God when the last vestige of personal attachment to lesser things and lesser ideas falls away and leaves you naked, bodyless, mindless, formless, empty, and transparent. And yet you find that you are at peace, fulfilled, satisfied, empowered, and moving easily among the people and things of the world.

PARTNERSHIP WITH GOD

We are invited into full partnership and oneness with God. Oneness is the absolute truth. We are made of the Stuff of God, the Mind of God, and in the Image of God. God is all that we are, but we are not all that God is.

Partnership is not an absolute, but a relative term that is developed by choice. Oneness was God's choice. Partnership is our willing response.

Humanity has thought up every conceivable relationship with God according to human perceptions. They have thought of:

God as bargainer
God as rescuer
God as savior (Jesus)
God as parent (loving or punishing)
God as judge (wrathful, vengeful)
God as counselor (Elijah)
God as lover (Song of Solomon)
God as pursuer (Hound of Heaven)
God as friend (Elisha)

The kind of relationship we choose to develop with others is a reflection of the kind of relationship we are trying to develop with God. The kind of God we search out, or create in our minds, is a reflection of our relationship with ourselves.

Since we saw our parents as god figures when we were very small, and even into our adulthood, we tend to image God with the characteristics of our parents. If we were afraid of our parent, we create a fearful God. We constantly punish ourselves for real or imagined offenses in an effort to cleanse ourselves and no longer offend the parent-god.

Crucial to our image of God is our self-image. One with a poor self-image cannot imagine God loving them. This poor self-image is the bottom line of most of our ills. Anorexia is a mind set that will not allow the child to eat and be nourished. The ultimate goal of the anorexic state of mind according to Peggy Jan-Pierre of Canada, is not a smaller dress size, but to disappear entirely. It is a death wish. The goal of drug users is to feel acceptance. On and on it goes throughout all the ills of society.

BEING GOD

Being God isn't something that you act out. It isn't a function of the ego nature. It isn't simply being someone else's idea of perfection. It isn't assuming that you are the totality of God.

It is knowing that God is all of you, every part. It is making God a part of all the secret places in yourself. It is living in the Presence of God whether you are shopping, making love, or praying. It is all the same.

Being God is simply walking "in the courts of the Lord" in your mind and not leaving them. Revelation states, "You shall go into the courts of the Lord and go no more out." Worrying about nothing. Fearing nothing. Being God is being the perfect reflection of Divine ideas manifest in your life. It is having your mind locked upon the appropriation of Divine Ideas and their perfect manifestation in your life.

CHRIST IN YOU

Divine Ideas are the perfect patterns for life that come from God Mind. The Christ nature is God's perfect pattern for humankind. Abundance is the perfect pattern for our sustenance. Health is the perfect pattern for our vehicle of expression, body, mind, and emotions. Wisdom is the perfect pattern for the direction of creation.

How can we attain all this? As I mentioned earlier, it isn't something we do, or strive for in a physical way. It certainly isn't something we worry or feel guilty about. It is what we endeavor to align our thoughts with as our ideal, an attainable goal only through the Christ nature.

Goodness is the nature of God, expressing in Divine Ideas, always available for our appropriation for our lives. Goodness is the nature of God that we trust, and love is the result.

NOT GOD

The world of humanity has long been full of fear about God. It came from the earthly elements that often killed people and wiped out what little civilization they had. Anything of cataclysmic proportions must surely be the wrath of the gods. Even our insurance companies used to call these events "Acts of God" and therefore uninsurable.

We no longer believe that the thunder is God, or the sun or moon. Everything in form is an out-picturing of God through the Divine Ideas into manifestation. One of those Divine Ideas is the Christ. Jesus, as a Christ, declared himself to be the father of all manifestation. We, in our original perfect vibrational Christ nature, created and manifested a world, an Earth school in which all things are part of our co-creator's laboratory and textbook.

As we "grow up into the head of Christ" (Ephesians 4:15) we become the likeness of God in consciousness. We are no longer just the hands and feet, the doing part. God is what we are through and through. We are aware of our God nature and manifest it in every part. In our language we are sons of God, children, priests, representatives, interpreters, and man-ifestors of God. We do not look for God at the point of manifestation, but as the Source of it. God is in the beginning and runs through our lives as the Original Pattern, the Divine Design that we are ascending to.

GOD

"I am that I am." No rationale, no excuses, no qualifiers, no argument, no discussion. "I AM" sent *you* as "I AM" sent Moses. You are sent as surely as you are here. You don't get here unless you are sent by God. Someone said that God doesn't choose the qualified. God qualifies the chosen. Our part is to choose God and in choosing God with every aspect of our being, our new name becomes "I AM."

Spiritual interpretation brings us to this place of acceptance. It weaves the Divine Design into our minds and lifts our understanding. It weaves our unique relationship to God upon the loom of our consciousness and belief, and our manifest lives are drawn upward.

Our response to our experience heightens. The highest response to God is co-creation with God. Partnership with God. The Book of Revelation characterizes it as the New Jerusalem, set forth in dazzling terms. The finite human mind cannot comprehend, but only aspires to this next dimension of being. Spiritual interpretation is the mental vehicle of our aspiration. It is a prayer of enormous dimension, scope, and potential. It is our highest response to the love of God.

MISCREATIONS JETTISONED

1. So, God is never angry with us? God is never angry with us. We are the angered ones.

We are the fearful ones who create an angry God when we are frustrated in our efforts to get what we want. We sputter away the divine energy in angry blasts and feel punished when we become empty. We are saved when we surrender in helpless despair, and God just naturally fills us up again. As we evolve spiritually we learn to use the divine energy in creative adventures, filling and replenishing as we go along.

2. So, God never judges us? God never judges us. God is law, something like electricity. The electricity serves us when we abide by its laws. It makes no

decisions about whether we are worthy or whether we are applying it for good. It responds when we flip the switch.

God's law is love. When we seek to understand the law of love, really understand at higher levels, we begin to bring ourselves into alignment with it. We must learn to know when we are not in tune, which is signaled by pain, and move our consciousness back into harmony with the law. We must discern the kind of thinking needed to accomplish that move and make the decision to do it.

The last and final judgment happens when we can look at our creations as truly co-creation with spirit and count it all good. We must be able to declare the presence of good just as God did in the Book of Genesis. God created and then declared, "It is very good!"

3. So, God never forgives us? God is aware only of the perfection that God created ... the "very good." There is nothing there for God to forgive. It is given to the son of man, according to Jesus, to forgive sins. We feel the pain, and we must forgive our own stuff. All that is not created of God is our stuff, our miscreations. We live with the consequences of them until we give them up for God! Forgive.

4. So, God did not create hell? We created hell. We created hellish thinking leading to miscreations that caused us pain, suffering and death. That is the one job that we can do better than God. We have created so much hell on this planet, that we are experts at it. We don't have to bother God with that one. God simply awaits our return to the state of Absolute Love, and it is up to us to choose the thoughts that will take us there.

5. You've guessed it already! We also create heaven. In fact that is the original intention, that we should bring forth the kingdom of heaven on earth. We do that by learning heavenly thinking and spiritual understanding. Earth is our school, our classroom. Once we learn to continually create heaven in the experience of our lives in this dimension, we will graduate to creating heaven's equivalent in the next dimension.

Our master teacher, the God Being we know as Christ Jesus, awaits us in the new classroom. Be well advised, friend, that we will not be allowed to take any of our hell into the next dimension. We must forgive and release it all before we can graduate. You must create the heavenly state of mind here and now.

6. Help! Is there any assistance? Any technical support available? Yes, there is. The deck is definitely stacked in our favor. God created us for success, and God is also our sustainer while we learn. Look again at the story of the Prodigal Son, spending his inheritance (creative substance) trying to learn how to live.

When we are jarred out of our pigpen illusions, we set our feet on the road toward the Father's house (God Mind). The son didn't travel very far before he was met, welcomed, given the robe of love, the shoes of understanding, the ring of wisdom, and domination over his mind, and escorted to the celebration.

The more you move in the right direction in mind, the more help you receive. You may struggle in your weakened state to get out of the pigpen, and it may seem like a huge effort at first, but the divine momentum of good soon picks up on your right-mindedness and carries you homeward.

ACTIVITY

This is a meditation toward a higher response. You can make your own meditation tape using it. While you copy meditation music onto another tape you dub your voice over the top of the music at the same time. Speak quietly and very slowly. Leave 2 or 3 seconds between phrases and perhaps 5 to 10 seconds between paragraphs. Your subconscious mind responds to your own voice and forms habits of thinking in new and higher ways.

I was born into a body. My body is not what I am.
I have emotions, but I am not my emotions.
I have thoughts, but they are not what I am.
I have experiences, but they do not define me.
I have opinions, but they do not lift me up.
I have perceptions, but they are only a point of view.

I am the inhabitor of a body.
I sense life through feeling responses.
I think as a framework for action.
I take action in my classroom of experience.
My body is a temple of God, and a vehicle for me.
My emotions power my thoughts into manifestation.
My thoughts seek to mirror God Thoughts.

My experiences lead me to inner healing.
My opinions dissolve and love comes forth.

In God.
I just am.
I am essence.
I am substance.
I am potential.
I am creativity.
I am action.
I am abundance.
I am wisdom.
I am love.
I am God's image.
I just am.
In God.

Into the world I came.
To bring the light of truth.
To light up the whole world.
To transmute fear into love.
To empower the good.
To act for God.
To be clear.
Without blemish.
Innocent.
I return to my Source.
With whom I am one.
Now.
Amen.

CHAPTER TWENTY SEVEN

CREATING THE NEW WORLD

"A whole new world … a new fantastic point of view. No one to tell us no or where to go, or say we're only dreaming. A whole new world …"

From Walt Disney's *Aladdin*

Former forty-first President George Bush declared a new world order. This was laughed at by his political opponents, but I did not laugh. Back to spiritual interpretation, I saw someone in the most powerful position in the world, the leader of the free world, declaring a new world order. I heard the universe announce through him what was coming. I don't know what he personally had in mind for a new world order, but that wasn't what was important to me. I am a spiritual interpreter of life, and to me it was a signal of great universal importance.

The United Nations began to emerge from a doubtful embryonic stage into functioning as an entity. Its members were still unwieldy, and full of their own politics and temporal power, but an alignment was emerging even in the face of disagreement. Countries were joining each other in the cause of world peace and humanitarian efforts. Yes, I know part of that was Desert Storm and other stormy events, but like a growing child, humanity is not mature yet. It is still growing up.

I saw and heard Mikhail Gorbachev speak in Fulton, Missouri, from the same platform and podium as Winston Churchill. When it was over, I ran up and placed my hands on that podium, and my feet on that platform, where the beginning and the ending of the cold war era were signaled. I wanted to stand on that threshold, too, physically as well as in consciousness, to embody the whole cycle that had just completed itself. I wanted to bless and acknowledge our evolutionary ongoing at that moment and place.

The clashing of opposites is being softened: freedom and oppression, hot and cold war, poverty and plenty, masses and individualism, isolation and universality.

We lifted our noses from the grindstone and turned our eyes toward space. From there the differences, borders, and nationalities disappeared and a beautiful seamless blue and white planet emerged into our sight for the first time.

A popular song said, "From a distance you look like my friend, and all the world is one. From a distance God is watching us ..." Yes, from a distance, out of reach of our ego issues, from a higher place where the Truth is evident. We are one planet, one people, one spirit, one creation, one life, one love. The rest, the ugliness and separation, are what we miscreated out of our fear and ignorance.

The good news is this: if we made this mess, we can unmake it. If from God's perspective we look like friends, then we can choose to actually be friends. If we are all created out of God Stuff and we are the creators of our lives every day, then we can choose to create a whole new world. But, we can't do it by abandoning our planet and leaving the mess behind. We will simply make another mess elsewhere because we have not learned. We have to first turn inward where it all comes from and declare a new order in our own thinking.

ABOUT YOURSELF!

1. What is your present state of mind? Happy, disappointed, sad, fearful, wary, angry, suspicious, confident, content, enthusiastic? You may have a combination depending upon what is manifesting in your life at the moment. Simply observe it. Perhaps jot it down.

2. What stages has your life gone through? Here you will need to go back over your history, perhaps sketch an outline of your life story to see the turning points where things changed and changed again. Do you remember the events that signaled that change? This will help you see that you've grown and moved through thresholds of learning about yourself.

3. What personal world do you live in now? Can you describe it?
   How are your relationships with others?
   What is the state of your health?
   What is the state of your prosperity?
   What message is your life carrying to others?
   Where do you want it to go from here?

4. Your life is your practice ground, your field placement, and your textbook. We await a knight in shining armor, a savior king, the hero or heroine to rescue us from whatever we are. We want an outer force that will step in and sweep us off into paradise, and away from the struggle. No one, though, can rescue us from what is inside.

There is an old story about a wagon train that was approaching a town. The elders of the town came out to meet it and asked the people where they had come from. The head of the wagon train said that they all came from a place full of thieves, murderers, and liars, and they were looking for better people to settle with. The elders replied that the wagon train should move on then, because they would surely find the same people here.

We bring with us what is inside, and we unconsciously recreate the same wherever we go. We want to examine what is inside so we know what we do not want to recreate. Then we can consciously choose what we truly desire to create.

BEGINNING OUR NEW WORLD

Please understand that the same energy with which you have created your unhappiness and failures is available to create the opposite. The energy doesn't care what you create with it. It simply responds to the form you imagine for it. In this way, you are totally recyclable.

Anger energy is simply energy used for anger. A psychologist asked me where I would be without my anger. I said, metaphorically, back in my hometown, married to the guy who runs the grocery store. I would not have visited all of the places and accomplished the things that I have. I eventually learned to use that energy, not to be angry, but to fuel my ambition to discover more about life, to find answers, and make something of myself.

Begin by reclaiming your energy from habitual emotional patterns and redirecting it toward efforts of a transformational quality. For instance, someone asked me if I get nervous before a speaking engagement. I answered that nervousness is an abundance of energy coming through me and I can choose anxiety or excitement. It awaits my choice. I choose to be excited.

My self-talk would be, "I choose to be excited. This is what I love to do. Thank you, God!"

I traded my anger energy for clarity of thinking and a plan or strategy for myself. I am not happy when I am angry, but I am happy when I direct energy toward creating a plan for success.

My self-talk would be, "I choose to make a plan where I can channel myself into ways of being that please me and bring success."

The trick is to be aware of what you are feeling in any given moment. Feelings are created by thoughts and we can choose to change or re-channel our feelings by rerouting our thinking. This is difficult because we habitually ignore our feelings until they are so powerful that we express them in destructive ways that make a mess of our world. Then we excuse our mess by declaring that we were right, we were entitled to be angry, or we couldn't help it (the devil made us do it).

AWARE AND FREE TO CHOOSE

Practice, practice, practice conscious deliberate manifestation of some creation in your mind. How can we trust ourselves to create the new world if we can't stay with an idea until we manifest it? We give up too easily. Look for the mindset that matches what you want and concentrate on it.

Start easy. Set your mind upon manifesting something you know is within your grasp, or have had already … like five bucks, like a parking place in a busy lot when you need it. Make a game of it and see how many times in a row you can make it happen.

Count five happy events each day at your home or office. It could be a compliment at lunch, an appreciative phone call, or help getting into the elevator. Perhaps this is small stuff, but if you can't get the small stuff to happen reliably, how will you do the big stuff? "When you are faithful over a few, I will set you over many." Matt.25:21

Your mind is a natural problem solver. It is constantly in motion solving problems. If it doesn't have a problem to solve, it will make one up. Oh, great! Having your mind make up problems just to have something to work on is just what you need, right?

But wait, this is good! This is exactly the machinery you want to have working for you. Something that is reliable and never quits. So you give your mind good challenges to work on such as five happy events each day. Soon your mind will be helping you create your new world instead of repeating the old problem patterns just for exercise.

But can't I just ask God for a good life and forget all this work? Yes, but once again it is your mind that welcomes or blocks the Divine Ideas that bring your good. If you are not in the habit of creating good thought patterns for your life, you are not going to be in the habit of receiving them either. So God will send you all good, which is all that God does anyway, and you will be on the wrong frequency. How much good have you blindly passed by in your life already? Tons of it! But don't look back. Begin now.

GOOD IS FOR US AND EVERYONE

We think we have experienced good. Yes, good happens as the bumper sticker says. But what we now know as good is miniscule when compared to what is possible. We have only scratched the surface.

We have accepted as good the bit of happiness and joy that the world has told us we can expect. But we are not to expect too much, and certainly not more than the world thinks is our share. After all, look at all the misery in the world.

It is because there is so much misery in the world that we must reach for greater and greater good. If our children are hungry, do we go hungry in honor of their hunger, or do we get food for them?

There is so much misery because people don't know that good exists for them or that they deserve only good. They don't know they are supposed to be happy. They have come to believe that it is somehow virtuous to be sober and without an abundance of good. They will even shun good, choosing misery, because they think that this is the will of God.

Once I participated in a discussion about whether we can play while others are in want. Can we enjoy life without guilt when the world is at war? I say we must! If the world chooses not to play, or doesn't know how to play, then we must be the example. If we give it up in some kind of sympathetic gesture, then it disappears from the world's stage. Then there is no hope, no example to lift others up. There is no encouragement for the world to give up the belief in misery as a way of life.

Reaching our "final frontier" means bringing spiritual joy into all life experience. We are spiritual beings descending upon the planet to bring the good news of God. It is our mission and purpose as extensions of God into earthly life.

Soaring over mountains
Striving to land;
Reaching through time
With an outstretched hand.

To grasp and to guide,
Through a hazy approach,
A starship comes calling
A new world to coach.

To learn a new game plan,
To find a new way;
A beacon, a welcome
I'm coming to stay.

> Whatever the challenge,
> We laugh and we share;
> Til joy is the lesson,
> And happiness not rare!
>
> Author

We often make a landing in different circumstances in life. We can shock those we suddenly join by exploding onto the scene with all the goodies we bring dumped out all at once. We find ourselves soaring in our spirituality, and we look like a starship landing to those around us. In our new excitement and enthusiasm we need to approach gently the scenes of our lives, new and old. We're learning a new game plan, but it still needs to fit into the world in which we live every day.

If we land too abruptly, others may reject us and be uncomfortable around us. It could severely disrupt relationships. That could cause some doubt about the practicality of your new-found spirituality. We must not doubt our spiritual nature and our part in the grand design. Nor must we settle down into miniscule good and call it enough. Rev. Jack Boland, Unity Minister, said many times, "Don't let your good get in the way of your greater good." This doesn't mean turn your back on or chase away your present good. It means steady progress toward greater good.

Stretch your mind and reach out into uncharted potential for greater patterns of good. God's good is absolute and limitless. We have an eternity to bring forth all the good God intended for us. We've barely begun. It is a joyous journey. Joy is the lesson, a happiness rare! We don't indulge in joy and happiness nearly enough.

WE ARE BEING SHOWN

How did we get from a single cell to the multidimensional, self-observing, co-creating godlings that we are? We've come a long way baby! We have gone from imperceptible movement to warp speed, watts to gigawatts and we've only just begun.

God shows us that we are in motion through the ability to look back over the history of mankind, the evolution of species, and even our own yesterdays. Where was your life five, ten, twenty years ago? Have you moved in your thinking, grown up and become wiser? Do you even resemble who you were back then? Probably not. Far from it.

We are shown the past, not to dwell upon it, or make it our future, but to perceive movement and growth. How else will we measure our progress? All I have to do when I am feeling stuck is think about where I was thirty years ago. The dark ages in my life. Despairing and lonely. Floundering. Now I look at my life today and find it is fulfilling and transforming in so many ways.

ASK TO SEE

Ask to have your perception cleared and expanded. Ask to see more advanced designs for being. Ask to see the next dimension that Jesus was speaking of when he was asked where he was going. Always ask to see the next step, and the next. Don't be bashful or think you are arrogant for wanting to know. God's business is your business, as the twelve-year-old Jesus said to his parents. "Did you not know that I must be about my Father's business?" You are invited to partake in as much as you can handle at any given time.

Marcus Bach describes something like this in his book, W*hat's Right With The World*. He writes, "It was an awareness, a sensitivity to a cosmic overlife—silent, mystic, an inner journey. A response to something ... that is to remain beyond. The totality of God remains forever beyond us, and yet ever available to us."

Even the most barren of deserts is teeming with life and potential. The Dead Sea isn't really dead. It doesn't have plant or animal life that we can see, but it is rich in mineral deposits. So rich in fact, that there are many industries around it drawing out its riches. I was amazed at its beauty when I saw it. It was dancing in the sun, and it inspired my poetry once again.

"Diamonds In The Dead Sea"

The place is dead they tell us.
The water holds no life.
The minerals have choked the land.
A dusty, barren land.

But I see diamonds on the sea.
The sparkling surface laughs.
And dances midst the earthen stripes.
A dusty, barren land.

I float above the deepest earth.
The green of change sublime.

> And touch the healing mud and sand,
> Of a dusty, barren land.
>
> Author

Even a dusty barren land is full of potential. The water was so dense with minerals that we couldn't sink, but bobbed like corks. And it was the color of a clear green emerald. The surface sparkled like diamonds, a huge field of diamonds. The mud is used for healing, as well as the water. Life and life-giving.

When you think you have run dry of ideas, ask God for more. When you can't see what is ahead, ask for the vision to see. When you need the right vibrational energy to accomplish something, ask God for it. Ask to see, ask to know, ask to be more! It is there for you as surely as the riches of the desert and the Salt Sea.

ACTIVITY

This is a turn-style chapter, a time to let go and a time to begin. It is a transition from where you've been to where you are going.

1. Glance over your personal story that you wrote after the first chapter. It is time to thank it for being your story and for bringing you to this moment. It has been a mixture of your mis-creations and your past, which was influenced by others. It was your practice ground and your waking up to something better. Now, it is time to bid it farewell and to let it go.

2. Now look over your cosmic story. How does it feel to you now? Does it still serve your purpose? Is it still large enough? Is there anything missing or that needs expanding?

Take the time now to do any additions to, any rearranging or touching up of your cosmic story that you think is necessary. This will be a frame for your new design. The next chapter will help you fill in more of the practical details and needed components. Don't give up. Keep working on it. Life is a work in progress, always.

CHAPTER TWENTY EIGHT

CHOOSING THE NEXT DESIGN

"The floodgates of my mind had opened. It was as if an unseen intelligence was infiltrating the memory bank of my brain, selecting ideas that had been stored through the years of experience. I organized nothing. I though of nothing. I simply followed the stream of ideas."

Barbara Marx Hubbard
The Revelation

From your past to writing your cosmic story has been a journey in learning all you could about yourself and your life experiences. Your cosmic story has been training wheels for the next step in spiritual evolution. Many questions have been asked in these former chapters to expand thinking. One skill we need is to be able to ask greater and more expanded questions than we've ever asked before. In creating the next Design, even greater questions must be asked. Creating a new humanity means we must now step out of the past, and the way we've always thought about things. The only path to that new and wonderful way is to ask.

Are there choices to be made in the next dimension of being? What choices can we possibly make for a world we do not yet know? Are they even ours to make?

Pierre Teilhard de Chardin, in *The Phenomenon Of Man* said that we are on the leading edge of our own spiritual evolution. We are not pushed by our biology, but beckoned and invited by the Creator, the Omega, the Ultimate Absolute of Creation.

How did we know what to create in this present dimension? Where have our ideas come from? How are they implemented? Divine Ideas are an inheritance from God. They flow to us, so to speak, constantly. They are bytes of God's wisdom that we can apprehend with the human mind, comprehend and bring into our life experience for our highest good.

This is why several people tap into the same idea at the same time. The middle to late 1800's saw the birth of new thought schools and churches all across our country, Europe, and Russia. The Fillmores, Ernest and Fenwick Holmes, Nona Brooks, Mary Baker Eddy, Phineas Parkhurst Quimby, Tielhard de Chardin, Leo Tolstoy, and Swedenborg are a few of the well known ones. There were many spiritual teachers who quietly conducted their own private schools and published their own books on their lessons of mind science and healing.

If our Creator/Sustainer has supplied us so richly in this dimension, we will not be deserted in the next as we continue on. Jesus said he was going "to prepare a place for us" in the next experience in living. At that time he said we, as humanity, weren't prepared to follow him, but we would eventually be, if we believed in and practiced the things he told us about it. The Apostle Paul took it a little further when he said, "Grow up into the head of Christ." That Christ consciousness within each of us has what it takes.

Strange, but maybe the easiest place to start making these decisions is with what we don't want in the next dimension. We usually know better what we don't want in our lives than what we do want. I have thought of paper work, credit cards, pollution, starvation, isolation, hatred, sickness, poverty and stupidity, for openers. When we look at our "don't wants," we can perhaps turn to the flip side of them for a clue. Intelligence, abundance, clarity, fulfillment, health ... it works both ways. We can begin to put our ideals into spiritual terms.

I have always been a *Star Trek, The New Generation* fan. The advanced thinking of Gene Roddenberry put us well along the road to thinking beyond our present realities. We have the equivalent of the silver screen in our minds, and a projector, a faculty called imagination. We can project new images upon the screen of our minds, leaving out what we don't want, and freeing ourselves to progress in what we do want and beyond.

LET'S TRY!

1. How will you enter the new realm?
—Will you have a body?
—Will you wear clothes?

I think I would like to ascend in consciousness to where I can have a transformed body of light rather than be born an infant and take thirty years to mature. Since the book of Corinthians says we are transformed from glory into glory, or dimension to dimension, I see myself becoming lighter, brighter, and able to shift my vibrational level at will. I will appear and disappear instead of being born and dying.

2. How will you communicate?
—Will you speak?
—Will you have a voice?
—Mind to mind?

I can see us as beings who merge thinking patterns and who co-create new patterns together. There need be no secrets because we have ascended out of the need for pain and darkness. We have ascended into the realm of love and acceptance, and readily lavish it upon each other.

We will share ideas instead of opinions. If there are struggles, they will be to see the greater picture. They will be to open to greater and greater wisdom. Each struggle culminates in success. Breakthroughs will dawn simultaneously upon the thought patterns of everyone who is ready.

3. What about having children?
—Will you have your own family?
—Will you need to protect your child from anything?

We will co-create a divine child the same way we bring forth any other Divine Idea. We will create a beautiful place for another soul to inhabit, give it the best that we are and have. We will love and nurture it carefully through each stage of its development. We will be honored to care for a godling emerging into our midst.

4. What about sex?
—Will there be male and female?
—Will we have just one partner?
—What about fidelity?

What sparks the urge to merge? The best idea I have heard so far comes from Barbara Marx Hubbard in her *Book Of Co-creation*. Her term is suprasex! The merging comes through being so excited about an idea that the interaction produces ecstasy. We can procreate with a very limited number of people, but co-creating is unlimited.

Two souls may choose to continue to co-create together, continuing to weave their ideas together in ever more wonderful patterns. Fidelity to the Divine Design and Divine Purpose always satisfies the longing for faithfulness and trust.

5. What about government?
—Who will rule this realm?
—Will we choose how we will be governed?

As ascended beings we are individually and wholly responsible for the expression of Spiritual Principle as our governing force. When one completely governs from the Christ Principle within, everything works out harmoniously for the highest good of all. Other than the perfect governing principle of spirit, what else would we need except perhaps a melody or melodies that we could all soul-sing together.

6. What about God?
—Will we know God more intimately?
—Will God be visible?

God is, always has been, and always will be the First Cause, Creative Principle. God is the Grand Impersonal made personal through us.

Here we get into what we have called the abstract. In the present dimension we want everything to be "concrete," in form, dense, touchable, inert, and solid. This idea makes us feel comfortable and safe in our three-dimensional world and thinking.

Eventually, we find ourselves no longer satisfied by this idea and look for something with more potential. We look for a way out of limitation and a way to advance somehow. There was a salamander on the window ledge of my mother's car. I tried to shoo it off, but it kept running toward the mirror mounted on the door. Over and over it ran into the mirror, the illusion of freedom, only to be thwarted again and again. Finally, I placed a book I was carrying in front of the mirror, and the salamander scampered down the door to freedom.

In our fourth dimensional way of being, we no longer hide in the illusion of form, but discover our safety in the unformed. The absolute. The invisible.

In the past we have created God in our human image and likeness. We gave God gender, voice, emotion, opinion, victory and vengeance, jealousy and parenthood. Now we must recreate God as our self-image changes and the Christ emerges. Seeing the invisible at last, the Christ Pattern, as our reality, we know the body, intellect and emotions as a temporary vehicle. We more easily conceptualize the invisible God, the Principle, the First Cause. The abstract is no longer remote, but a very intimate and real life force within us as us.

WE KNOW WHERE HOME IS

We innately know where home is because God is within us at all times. There is a still small voice that speaks to us continually and we must remember how to listen. It is often referred to as following our bliss. Bliss is a little explosion of joy, like silent fireworks in the night sky. It happens when we are totally on track. It is usually a split second happening because our intellect quickly takes hold and classifies it as an emotional experience or fantasy of not much value.

We are beginning to discover the difference between feeling and emotion. The feeling nature draws our attention toward the invisible, the eternal. Emotion draws us toward the physical and quickly burns us out. The "voice" of God is a feeling, an intuition, a shift, an expansion, an empowerment, a lifting. The feeling nature is a spiritual receiver. Emotion is a physical experience.

In the garden Easter morning, Jesus said to Mary Magdalene, "Why do you weep?" Why are you having a physical experience instead of a spiritual one? I have taught you to be a healer, teacher, transformer, and when I reveal to you the greatest achievement of all, you drop back into the physical/emotional state! "Go, find the disciples and tell them I have risen!" Go to all the faculties within you and tell them you are now a new being in Christ.

As Jon Luc Picard said every week on *Star Trek, The New Generation*, "Space, the final frontier!" From deep within the density of the earth to the awesome power of the ocean, to the vast and seeming nothingness of space, we have mirrored for ourselves the depth and breadth of our inner kingdom.

In the transporter room of our inner being, we will dematerialize our limitations and travel unhindered to whatever dimension calls us to explore it. We will truly "go where no one has gone before" because it is not only in human form that we go there, but in the essence and expansiveness of godlikeness.

In the consciousness of godlikeness we are offered eternal life, not to be confused with sitting on a cloud playing a harp, but actually exploring God. In Malachai 3:10 it is written, "Put me to the test ..." We are invited to test and explore every dimension of God.

The quote goes on, "... and see if I will not open the windows of heaven ..." You will see and co-create heaven everywhere. "... And pour out for you a blessing so great you will not be able to contain it!" You will love this experience with such a vast love that you will have to constantly give it away.

And so, dear friend, we launch ourselves into the next stage of existence. Revelation called it "the New Jerusalem." Jesus called it "many mansions." The Book of Corinthians calls it "changing from glory into glory." Language as we know it is limited in its ability to express the higher experiences. We try to put Divine revelation into words and explanations that always sound a little crazy. But keep talking! A new language is already emerging. We are creating the words, the mental technology, and the spiritual super highway that carries us inward and upward.

We create the Divine Design of our own being as we go along. God is fascinated to experience the design through us, as us. God conceived creation and man is the man-ifestor of God in form. Man is the chooser, spearhead, and co-creative partner with God. Man, in Sanskrit, means hand.

We are the hand of God stretching forth through eternity into creation so that God can experience as well as BE. Our ultimate fulfillment comes in knowing and living our godlikeness to the greatest extent we can conceive, reaching out in our thinking to know more and ultimately be more. "Is it not written in your law, 'I said you are gods'?" John 10:34

EPILOGUE

This is the Pathway;
Tread light, heart and feet.
Venture forth now today,
Stepping, drumming the beat.

Our future is rising,
Our present to unfold.
The gifts of the Unknown,
Are a treasure of gold.

Lightening and brightening,
We are called home within,
O'er a widening horizon,
Where all new we begin.

Our hands remain empty,
When filled with this light.
I carry no burden.
I move with delight.

Touch down, fly away.
We're both here and there.
We're in Godness today
And in God, everywhere!

Author

I believe you can really make a transformation within yourself by spiritually interpreting your life. This is your jumping off place to begin a cosmic journey far more amazing than the life you have lived so far. Yesterday was but a dream because we were asleep. Our reality begins now because we are awake. If you have read the last chapter first, as many do, you will find all the more reason to begin at the first chapter and do the work.

If you have completed this book and all it asks you to do, you are forever changed as I am for having lived it and written it. To discover this pathway was my first major shift. To teach it in lessons, classes, and every day living was a great and glorious journey. To write about it has been another level of expansion in my own explorations.

Perhaps my efforts will give you a "leg-up" on the next creative expression of our likeness to God. As we meet together in consciousness and share in ever-higher ways, may we dwell in joy and ecstasy in the next dimension of which Jesus spoke. Over two thousand years later, we may at last be ready to reply, "We are ready! Here we come!"

Great Blessings To You,

Carole M. Lunde

ABOUT THE AUTHOR

Rev. Carole M. Lunde is a Unity minister. She was born in Mantua, Ohio, and attended Ashland College, Ashland Ohio. She holds a bachelor's degree in Interpersonal Communication and a master's degree in Counseling from Western Michigan University. She was graduated from Unity School of Christianity, Unity Village, Missouri, in 1985 and ordained in her first church in Columbia, Missouri, in 1986.

She has worked in the business and helping professions, and has been a minister for twenty two years. She has been a dedicated worker for world peace, and for the transformation of people's lives.

In 1990 she received the Susan N. Krauss award from Global Family in recognition of her service to global peace. She traveled with Global Family to Russia, Georgia, Ukraine, and the Czech Republic. She has also traveled to Israel and Egypt. On the second of her trips to Russia, she had a unique opportunity to teach in a school of philosophy in St. Petersburg, Russia.

She served three Unity Churches over the last 22 years, Columbia, Missouri, San Jose, California, and presently Lincoln, Nebraska. She has two sons, and currently lives in Lincoln, Nebraska.

BIBLIOGRAPHY

There are many wonderful spiritual/metaphysical books in print. I have chosen the few I have read that deal specifically with the spiritual interpretation of your life, or they have inspired me to look at mine in more expanded ways. You may in turn find others.

1. Carey, Ken: *Return Of The Bird Tribes; Harper Collins* 1988
2. Fillmore, Charles: *Atom Smashing Power Of Mind;* Unity School Of Christianity, 1949
3. Fillmore, Charles: *The Metaphysical Bible Dictionary;* Unity School of Christianity, 1931
4. Holmes, Ernest: *This Thing Called Life;* G.P.Putnam's Sons, 1948
5. Hubbard, Barbara Marx: *The Revelation. The Book Of Co-creation: Our Crisis Is A Birth;* Nataraj; 1995
6. Hubbard, Barbara Marx: *The Evolutionary Journey A Personal Guide To A Positive Future;* Evolutionary Press of the Institute for the Study of Conscious Evolution; 1982.
7. Rodegast, Pat & Stanton, Judith: *Emmanual's Book, A Manual For Living Comfortably In The Cosmos*; Simon & Schuster, 1985.
8. Sarkin, Annalee, *Ye Are Gods;* DeVorss & Co.; 1952
9. Zukov, Gary: *The Seat Of The Soul* (1989)

978-0-595-43974-4
0-595-43974-8

Printed in the United States
92053LV00003B/337-366/A